'Environmental security is one of these poisonous concepts which cloud the mind. Jon Barnett has now dissected the concept, revealing its baleful impact on our thinking.'
Wolfgang Sachs, author of *Planet Dialectics* **and editor of** *The Development Dictionary*

'Environmental security is a key issue in the contemporary world, but for too long it has been just another way of arguing for traditional types of national security. Jon Barnett — clearly utterly in control of his material — offers an alternative view in which peace and justice are not regarded as add-on extras to environmental security but central to it. Barnett distinguishes provocatively between environmental and eco-logical security, and he writes persuasively about the kinds of institutions required to bring them about.'
Professor Andrew Dobson, Keele University

'Jonathan Barnett's examination and critique of the "meaning of environmental security" is one of the most detailed, far-reaching and perspicacious so far published. It should be required reading not only for those interested in peace and justice but also anyone who has or intends to conduct research in the field.'
Ronnie Lipschutz, Associate Professor of Politics, University of California, Santa Cruz

'Barnett marches straight into the lion's den of national security policy, and walks out with a tame security policy firmly linked to a guarding of the environment in all its ecological complexity — and complete with human need as a key feature of that complexity. This is an amazing feat and unlocks a whole new set of strategies for peace scholars and activists who have long struggled to delink human security from militarized state security. Risky? Yes. Opening up creative new pathways for social change? Yes. An adventurous book for adventurous peacemakers.'
Elise Boulding, Professor Emerita of Sociology, Dartmouth College and former secretary general of the International Peace Research Association

'Concern about environmental threats to security now permeate many international policy discussions in Europe and North America. This powerful critique shows how conventional thinking about environmental security relies on a combination of ethnocentrism and Malthusianism to obscure both the causes and consequences of global environmental degradation and human insecurity. By putting the practical lived experiences of peoples, rather than the military prerogatives of powerful states, at the heart of a reformulated environmental security, Jon Barnett offers a construc-tive alternative that moves the policy debate ahead.'
Simon Dalby, Associate Professor, Carleton University, and Coeditor of Environment and Security

About the Author

Dr Jon Barnett researches and teaches at the MacMillan Brown Centre for Pacific Studies, University of Canterbury. He was educated at Melbourne University before doing his doctorate at the Centre for Resource and Environmental Studies at the Australian National University. He has contributed to various scholarly journals and has written chapters for a number of edited volumes on the issue of environmental and national security. He adopts a critical Green perspective to interrogate global politics and environmental politics and policy. This is his first book.

Zed Books Titles on Conflict, Security and International Relations

A. Adedeji (ed.), *Comprehending and Mastering African Conflicts: the Search for Sustainable Peace and Good Governance*

T. Allen and J. Seaton (eds), *The Media of Conflict: War Reporting and Representations of Ethnic Violence*

C. Cockburn, *The Space Between Us: Negotiating Gender and National Identities in Conflict*

S. Fisher *et al.*, *Working with Conflict: Skills and Strategies for Action*

N. Guyatt, *The Absence of Peace: Understanding the Israeli–Palestinian Conflict*

Bjorn Hettne *et al.*, *International Political Economy: Understanding Global Disorder*

Terence Hopkins and Immanuel Wallerstein *et al.*, *The Age of Transition: Trajectory of the World System, 1945–2025*

S. Jacobs, R. Jacobson and J. Marchbank (eds), *States of Conflict: Gender, Violence and Resistance*

K. Koonings and D. Kruijt (eds), *Societies of Fear: the Legacy of Civil War, Violence and Terror in Latin America*

L. Lumpe (ed.), *Running Guns: the Black Market in Small Arms*

Linda Melvern, *A People Betrayed: the Role of the West in Rwanda's Genocide*

J. Salmi, *Violence and Democratic Society*

Michael Schulz, Fredrik Soderbaum and Joakim Ojendal (eds), *Regionalization in a Globalizing World: a Comparative Perspective on Forms, Actors and Processes*

M. Suliman (ed.), *Ecology, Politics and Violent Conflict*

M. Turshen and C. Twagiramariya (eds), *What Women Do in War Time: Gender and Conflict in Africa*

J. Vickers, *Women and War*

For full details of this list and Zed's other subject and general catalogues, please write to:
The Marketing Department, Zed Books, 7 Cynthia Street, London N1 9JF, UK or email Sales@zedbooks. demon. co.uk

The Meaning of
Environmental Security

Ecological Politics and Policy
in the New Security Era

Jon Barnett

Zed Books
LONDON AND NEW YORK

The Meaning of Environmental Security: Ecological Politics and Policy in the New Security Era
was first published in 2001 by
Zed Books Ltd., 7 Cynthia Street, London N1 9JF, UK and
Room 400, 175 Fifth Avenue, New York, NY 10010, USA

Distributed in the USA exclusively by Palgrave, a division of
St Martin's Press, LLC, 175 Fifth Avenue, New York, NY 10010, USA.

Cover design by Andrew Corbett
Designed and set in 10/12 pt Monotype Bembo
by Long House, Cumbria, UK
Printed and bound in the United Kingdom
by Biddles Ltd, Guildford and King's Lynn

A catalogue record for this book
is available from the British Library

US CIP has been applied for

ISBN   Hb 978 1 85649 786 2
        Pb 1 85649 786 0

Transferred to Digital Printing in 2008

Contents

Abbreviations

ADF	Australian Defence Force
AODRO	Australian Overseas Disaster Response Organisation
CIA	Central Intelligence Agency (US)
COGG	Commission on Global Governance
CO2	Carbon Dioxide
DOD	Department of Defense (US)
DOE	Department of Energy (US)
DPIE	Department of Primary Industries and Energy (Australia)
DUSD(ES)	Deputy Under Secretary of Defense (Environmental Security) (US)
EPA	Environmental Protection Agency (US)
GDP	Gross Domestic Product
HDI	Human Development Index
HEE	Human Energy Equivalent
ICPD	International Conference on Population and Development
IPCC	Intergovernmental Panel on Climate Change
IPRA	International Peace Research Association
NATO	North Atlantic Treaty Organisation
NGO	Non Governmental Organisation
NSS	National Security Strategy (US)
ODA	Official Development Assistance
OPEC	Organisation of Petroleum Exporting Countries
SEI	Strategic Environment Initiative (US)
SERDP	Strategic Environmental Research and Development Program (US)
UN	United Nations
UNCED	United Nations Conference on Environment and Development
UNCHS	United Nations Conference on Human Settlements
UNDP	United Nations Development Programme
UNEP	United Nations Environment Programme
US	United States
WCED	World Commission on Environment and Development
WHO	World Health Organisation
WRI	World Resources Institute

Acknowledgements

Many people were subjected to lengthy tirades over the period in which I wrote this book. In that I expounded my ideas much more than I listened, no-one can accept responsibility for any of the failings of this book. However, if there's something useful being said in this book, one of the people named below can probably claim responsibility.

One of the few people who has managed to get a word in is Stephen Dovers. Steve has always been generous with his time, patient, and a good friend. I would also like to thank Graeme Cheeseman, Lorraine Elliott, John Handmer and Henry Nix for their respective efforts. Michael Carr has been intellectually and alcoholically inspiring, challenging and entertaining.

Apart from a few (not genetic) character defects, my parents have prepared me well for the world and have maintained their confidence in me. Thanks to Dad and Cath for help with the computer. David and Jan Ellemor have been terrific proxy parents. Many others have also made the task of completing this book easier, including Mark Busse, Mick Common, Robin Connor, Simon Dalby, Fiona Ellis, Jason Evans, Phil Gibbons, Tony Hooper, Kate Jarman, Urs Koenig, Mick McCarthy, Doug Mills, Ueantabo Neemia-Mackenzie, Sara Norbury, Kirsten Parris, Damean Posner, Stuart Rees, Maria Ryan, Kate Scott, David Small, Michael Webber, Ian White, Bill Young, and Andre Zerger. Apologies to anyone I may have forgotten. Thanks to Robert Molteno and his colleagues at Zed Books, and to Mike and Kate Kirkwood of Long House for their editorial and production work.

I would particularly like to thank all those at the Centre for Resource and Environmental Studies at the Australian National University who were great support for most of the time it took to write this book. Thanks also to the Macmillan Brown Centre for Pacific Studies at Canterbury University and the New Zealand Foundation for Research, Science and Technology for support during 1999.

Finally, Heidi Ellemor has continually made me laugh. She has helped me be an adult and an academic without losing my humour, compassion, and playfulness. Her love and friendship cannot be acknowledged in mere words.

1

Locating Environmental Security

The increasing scientific and broader social recognition of environmental problems exposes and challenges the ecologically destructive nature of the modern world. Theories, discourses and practices of security are a cornerstone of the modern political and economic order. This book critically examines the collision of environment and security. In this sense it is a study of global environmental politics, but one embedded in an awareness of the many interrelated problems of late modernity. Thus the subject of environmental security is a reflection of broader political and social developments, particularly as they relate to environmental degradation and injustice.

The concept of environmental security has become increasingly popular since the end of the Cold War, but its meaning is by no means clear. The literature has evolved in an *ad hoc* manner with a variety of interpretations vying for credibility. Ambiguity and diversity are characteristics of this literature. Environmental security arises from the conjunction of two powerful yet (probably) ontologically divergent words: 'environment' and 'security'. Readers need scarcely be reminded that in the name of this amorphous 'security' inestimable amounts of life and spirit have been wasted – yet who has been secured and from what contingencies have they been saved? 'Environment' is no less elusive and its history may yet be no less malignant, as by virtue of its ambiguity and its intuitive resonance it is amenable to misuse to support interests which are the antithesis of the Green agenda. So, to pursue the question 'What is the meaning of environmental security?' is to explore certain theories and discourses which wind throughout modern politics and collide at the juncture of environment with security.

Despite the contested meaning of environmental security a policy discourse has emerged in the United States, although this discourse is itself far from clear about the meaning of environmental security. That environmental security is now informing policy obviates, so it is assumed, the need for an examination of the concept. In addition, there is increasing casual use of environmental security as an alternative to existing approaches, such as sustainable development, to assist in the comprehension and resolution of environmental problems. That existing approaches, however theoretically coherent and well intended, have failed (thus far) to lead to the resolution of most environmental problems makes the development of an alternative concept potentially useful. At present environmental security does not offer much of a contribution in this respect. A critical examination, however, and a more consistent reformulation may well help in the production of an environmental security concept that is better able to comprehend environmental problems and inform policy.

Where this book comes from

This book is critical of most existing discourses and resulting policies on environmental security. Critical in this sense means questioning established orders of knowledge and practice to expose those which impede the realisation of the good life. The perspective of the critique is a rough amalgam of various strands of critical thought, including the 'critical theory' of the Frankfurt School and feminist and poststructuralist international relations and geopolitics theory. But the main source of this book's critical disposition is Green theory, where the capital 'G' denotes the radical ecophilosophical perspective embodied in ecofeminsm and social ecology (see Zimmerman 1993 and Dobson 1992).

The particular Green theory applied in this book is consistent with what many would see as the core features of such an approach. First, there is a suspicion that modern anthropogenic and utilitarian cosmology is responsible for environmental degradation, seen to be inextricably connected to the 'political, social, economic and scientific consensus that dominates the late twentieth century' (Dobson 1992: 4). Second, there is a particular philosophy of space and scale, consistent with the Green maxim that 'everything is connected to everything else'. There is therefore a sensitivity to the complexity and interdependence within and between social and ecological systems: just as the individual is a synergistic component of the social, so the subatomic particle is an inextricable component of the biosphere; and just as the stand of trees in any local park has some ecological function in global terms, so does the British household have some function in the global economy. Green theory is also very much attuned to the problems of uncertainty and how to act in the face of incomplete or partial 'truths', and it is suspicious of 'facts' in the light of this pervasive uncertainty (Paterson 1996). In as much as this renders 'the boundary' – be it physical or conceptual – meaningless, Green theory is an exemplar of poststructural sensibility (Doran 1995).

Certain interrelated values, the most important of which are those of peace and justice, shape the moral domain within which the discourses and practices of environmental security are to be scrutinised in what follows. Thus the theory of this book can be said to be normative: a mode of theorising and critiqueing which explicitly acknowledges and purposefully deploys the beliefs and values of the theorist. Other examples might include the feminist value of freedom for women or the value of ecological sustainability in Green theory, and the normative theories used to expose practices which impede these values. Although contentious in certain academic circles, this type of critique is ubiquitous: 'we continuously uphold normative or value propositions that are entirely unproblematic and without doubt rational in every sense: children should not play with fire; fraud is unjust' (Morrow 1994: 239).

An explanation of this book's values is necessary because it makes the politics inherent in what follows more transparent. In this sense, then, the normative position being explicated here is not so much a self-evident universal truth as a starting point for the book and subsequent debate.

Peace and justice

There is no absolute or rigorous conception of peace that can be asserted to be better than another, but there is a general sense, supported by a degree of consensus, of what constitutes peace. Similarly, there will never be one optimal way to bring about peace; it requires a host of complementary concepts and strategies (one of which may be environmental security). Peace is integrally concerned with the elimination of violence, where violence is an act or process which impedes people from realising their potential (Galtung 1969). So violence is much more than causing physical harm (direct violence); it is also the absence of social justice and includes the monopolisation and manipulation of knowledge (indirect violence). Achieving peace is therefore very much about the melioration of power. In this way peace can be said to have both a negative and a positive dimension. Negative peace refers to the absence of direct violence that causes physical harm, and positive peace refers to the absence of structural violence manifested as the uneven distribution of power and resources.

Negative peace is reactive in nature in that it seeks the cessation of actual or impending conflict. This is most frequently understood as 'peace as the absence of war', enabling peace to be narrowly interpreted as 'anti-war' and creating a perverse logic of unreason whereby, through the idea of deterrence, military and strategic planners can refer to themselves as 'peace planners'. Positive peace, on the other hand, is proactive in nature. It seeks to remove the underlying structural imbalances that present risks and vulnerabilities to people in the short as well as the long term. Galtung (1969) notes that negative and positive peace are contiguous with each other, at least in theory. However, the competing uses of the word 'peace' in the twentieth century have made its meaning ambiguous; it can be, and is, deployed in ways that are very much anti-peace in the same way that 'environment' and 'security' can be deployed to legitimate practices that perpetuate environmental damage and insecurity.

Integral to a meaningful understanding of peace is an appreciation of justice. A difficult theoretical concept, justice is seen here not so much in terms of perfect equity in holdings, nor as total rectification of historical injustices (although a moderated implementation of these two aspects are important), but rather as the goal of greater equity among all people in the world. Neither scepticism about the possibility of absolute equity (absolute justice), nor the postmodern unmasking of the way universal claims about justice are a means by which some groups advance power over others, should compromise the validity of the goal of justice. Best seen as intellectual checks against the replacement of one undesirable state with another, these concerns should not impede progress towards a more just world, for there are clear disparities in life chances among people which are morally indefensible and demand action (these are discussed in the following chapter). Indeed, it is a perverse form of humanism that argues against the possibility of justice in the name of freedom and diversity.

Simply put, a minimum condition of peace and justice would be when everyone has their basic needs satisfied. The provision of certain basic needs such as civil liberties, housing, clean water and food can be seen as universal human rights. There is thus a continuity between peace, justice, basic needs and human rights, reflected in the International Human Rights Covenants where we find the most detailed, internationally sanctioned expression of the minimum requisite conditions for peace and justice (Donnelly 1993). The consensus of states, in this instance at least, confers legitimacy on these covenants. The principles of peace and justice are made clear enough in the two covenants on Civil and Political Rights and on Economic, Social and Cultural Rights. It is clear that the best means by which people can attain these rights is unfettered participation in shaping and reshaping their lives as they choose. The challenge today is less one of redefining these rights (although the inclusion of rights to resources and environmental services is arguably necessary), and more one of implementation.

In so far as peace is meaningless unless there is relative certainty about its provision, security is an important aspect of its formulation and delivery. In other words peace needs to be 'secured' against contingency. Conversely, security understood as a general state of stability and predictability is arguably necessary to implement a more peaceful social order. Peace is therefore an object of security, as well as a means by which security is obtained, as peace itself is the best way of ensuring security for the greatest number of people (Dower 1995). The nebulous subject of security is discussed in greater depth in Chapter 3.

A range of values are associated with the meta-values of peace and justice, including cooperation, diversity, equality, harmony, responsibility, trust, accountability, participation, and shared power (Gurtov 1991: 15). Peace also has resonance with environmental issues; for example, the Rio Declaration on Environment and Development recognised that 'Peace, development and environmental protection are interdependent and indivisible' (Principle 25, UNCED 1993). Nevertheless, the theory and practice of explicitly linking environmental issues and peace is not fully developed. The concept of environmental security is one means by which to further our understanding of the ways in which peace and environment are related.

Some definitional issues

For the sake of clarity it is necessary to define certain terms. This book talks of theory, concept and discourse. A *theory* is an attempt to explain an aspect of reality. Theory is approached in this book as a critical process which reflects on itself as much as on the reality to be explained. There is a clear distinction between this introspective critical approach to theory and that of the traditional (explanatory and predictive) positivist sciences.

A *discourse* is a specialist language which enables social power by describing the world in a particular way, and which makes possible certain claims to truth, hence justifying certain forms of action (Foucault 1977). In the way they depict the world, discourses fail to recognise the existence of certain aspects of reality (for example a neoliberal discourse fails to acknowledge the causes of poverty), and they may construct alternative truths (the neoliberal discourse argues that private sector growth will benefit the poor by the 'trickle down' effect, when experience provides little evidence for this). In so doing, discourses write out of consideration possible courses of action (the neoliberal discourse excludes the possibility of stronger state intervention to prevent poverty and protect the poor). In the realm of policy, discourses do not accurately explain that which they purport to know, yet they have considerable influence.

A *concept* is a general notion or idea with a particular although contestable meaning. A concept helps to explain, classify and organise thoughts, and concepts are frequently used in theories and discourses. Although concepts have basic meanings and intuitive resonances, many have competing interpretations. Concepts such as freedom, justice, liberty, security and sustainable development are all subjects of considerable debate. This book therefore refers to environmental security as a concept rather than as a discourse or a theory because it is, at present, a contested idea. The essential meaning of environmental security lies in the relationship between environmental degradation and security, but the details of this idea – the particular representation of the relationship – are the subject of debate. Thus it is most accurate to understand this book as an examination of the meaning of the concept of environmental security.

Where this book goes

The environmental security rubric can be seen to comprise several related sub-areas. These are displayed in Figure 1.1, a heuristic guide to the study of the concept which should be seen as a loose device to aid comprehension and not as an overly literal or accurate classification. It is intended to

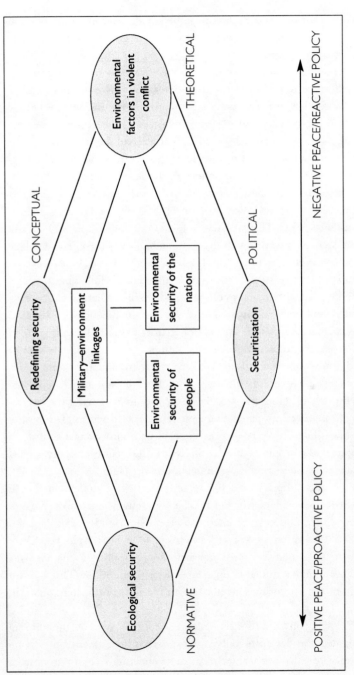

Figure 1.1 Environmental Security: A Heuristic Guide

serve as a cursory introduction to some key dimensions of the environmental security literature which are explored in greater depth throughout the remainder of this book.

The seven major areas comprising the environmental security agenda are: efforts to redefine security; theories about environmental factors in violent conflict; the environmental security of the nation; the linkages between the military and environmental issues; the ecological security agenda; the environmental security of people; and the issue of securitisation. These are discussed in turn in chapters 4 to 9, while the issue of securitisation is discussed throughout the book.

One of the pervasive silences associated with the concept of environmental security is its inverse, presumably present condition of environmental *in*security. That this state of environmental insecurity remains largely unexplored says much about the ambiguity of theories and policies on environmental security. This book offers a particular, human-centred account of environmental insecurity, outlined in the following chapter.

Because security is a key component of environmental security, there is a need to understand its meaning, which is the function of Chapter 3. This chapter discusses the concept of security in general terms, and then discusses and critiques the dominant nation-centred approach which has conditioned almost all existing accounts of environmental security.

Since at least the 1970s there have been a variety of attempts to redefine the meaning and practice of security so as to wrest the concept away from insecurity-generating national security practices. This push to redefine security gave rise to the concept of environmental security, as Chapter 4 explains. In Figure 1.1 this redefining security category is called the *conceptual rationale* for environmental security (after Soroos 1994).

From these efforts to redefine security has flowed an investigation (in retrospect inevitable) of the linkages between environmental degradation and conflict. This environment–conflict thesis considers that depletion and contamination of various resources, as well as rapid population growth, will induce violent conflict. Soroos calls this the *theoretical* dimension in that it focuses on cause–effects relationships. This aspect of environmental security is given considerable and critical attention in this book.

Following on from efforts to redefine security is the idea – not suprising given that the dominant purveyor of security in modern times is the nation-state – that national security can be undermined by environmental degradation. This is the locus of the strongest policy discourse associated with environmental security, and it is heavily informed by theories about environmentally induced conflicts. This is discussed in Chapter 6 with particular reference to US security policy, where it is argued that environmental security has been interpreted and deployed in ways that legitimise traditional security practices.

The fourth area of the environmental security rubric considers the links between the traditional agent of security, the military, and the environment. Beyond the rather obvious point that war causes environmental degradation, there is also consideration here of the way preparations for war degrade the environment, making militaries a significant cause of environmental insecurity. A more challenging area of inquiry here, one which Chapter 7 discusses in some detail, is the difficult question of whether militaries can have any positive role to play in enhancing environmental security.

The idea of ecological security, as distinct from environmental security, adopts a deep Green perspective by considering the biosphere as the penultimate referent of security. This area is called the *normative case*, and is discussed in Chapter 8 (Soroos 1994). Although undeveloped compared to other aspects of the environmental security rubric, the idea of ecological security implies an application of ecological theory to security. The question of whether the concept of ecological security is more or less useful than that of environmental security is also explored in Chapter 8.

The extension of a recent wave of thinking about human security to the subject of environmental degradation is the starting point for Chapter 9, where it is argued that environmental security needs to be human-centred, peace-oriented and adaptive to change in order to overcome the limitations (and omissions) of existing approaches. A human-centred environmental security concept combines the interests of peace and the environment, and it contests and contrasts with the dominant nation-centred and conflict-oriented approach. It also serves as an alternative paradigm from which new understandings and responses to environmental problems may emerge.

The most important underlying theme (and tension) in the environmental security literature is the (open-ended) question of the desirability of understanding environmental issues as security issues. Securitising environmental issues calls for extraordinary responses from governments equal in magnitude and urgency to their response to (military) security threats. Hence the identification of the final category (securitisation) which concerns the *political rationale* of environmental security (Soroos 1994). This securitisation issue pervades all of the literature and recurs throughout this book.

The last chapter of this book considers the implication of its critique, and its rewriting of environmental security as human security, for politics, policy and governance. This discussion does not propose detailed policy measures, arguing that these are available elsewhere. Instead, it addresses institutions of politics and governance, arguing that these are responsible for the failure to provide environmental security. The role of individuals as political agents is also considered. It is argued that national policy should foster dialogue between a more diverse range of interests represented in reformulated governance processes.

Establishing the links between each of these categories is an imprecise exercise. Such links are depicted in the heuristic guide, but their implications should not be overstated. The most salient point is the way in which redefining security and securitisation can lead to a focus on either national security or ecological security, and that these two referent objects are closely associated with a concern for conflict and a concern for human security respectively. The heuristic guide also implies a disjuncture between national and human security (no links), a reasonable assumption given their different ontological predispositions. Further, there is for the most part no connection between the theoretical concern about environmentally induced conflict and the ecological security approach. Finally, the category that considers the effects of the military in war and peace can also be linked analytically to both of these major constellations in the literature, but the link is generally not well made between this and the categories of redefining security and securitisation.

There is one other obvious feature of the heuristic guide presented in Figure 1.1: the depiction of a positive–negative peace continuum. Again, this should be regarded as a device to aid comprehension rather than a definitive classification. The continuum implies that those approaches that are concerned with conflict and national security adopt a negative peace/security perspective, and those that favour human security and ecological security adopt a positive peace/security approach. Attempts to redefine security, discussions of the impact of the military in war and peace, and the question of securitisation are all more or less neutral with respect to this positive–negative continuum (although the tone and implications of these tend to favour positive peace). Concomitant with this positive–negative continuum is a policy focus that favours proactive or reactive solutions.

2

Environmental Insecurity
Ecological Exacerbations
of Underdevelopment

A particular difficulty with environmental security is the absence of agreement on the problem that it is intended to address. In some respects environmental security is the answer to a question that was never asked (Brock 1997). It is important, then, to clarify the problematic of environmental insecurity. Latent in the different theories and discourses that abound are two principal ways of understanding the problem: as the threats to national security that arise from environmental degradation; or as the human impacts on the security of the environment itself (what this book refers to as ecological security). This book takes a different approach, understanding environmental insecurity to be the way in which environmental degradation threatens the security of *people*, with a particular emphasis on the differentiated impacts of environmental degradation on different groups of people. In this sense this approach to environmental insecurity has resonance with theories of environmental justice (see, for example, Bullard 1994).

Environmental insecurity is a function of the more general problem of environmental degradation. Environmental degradation is in turn a function of resource- and pollution-intensive forms of development coupled with poverty-driven rapid population growth. Hence environmental problems such as biodiversity loss, climate change, acid rain, and shortages of fresh water, food and fuelwood can all be seen as by-products of modern, particularly post-Second World War development practices and the social disparities they produce. So environmental insecurity cannot be fully understood in isolation from broader social, environmental and development trends.

The causes and effects of environmental degradation are spatially differentiated. It is in the service of industrialised areas that the bulk of resources are extracted and the bulk of the most damaging pollutants are produced. For example, the wealthiest 20 per cent of the world's population consume 84 per cent of all paper and 45 per cent of all meat and fish; they own 87 per cent of the world's vehicles and emit 53 per cent of carbon dioxide (UNDP 1998). The environmental impacts of this consumption, however, are spread across an area greater than the territory of industrialised countries; in effect their ecological footprint, like their economic footprint, is far greater than their sovereign domain. For example, while the industrialised countries are responsible for more than 60 per cent of carbon dioxide emissions, the climatic effects are felt by all people; indeed, as this chapter explains, the impacts tend to be felt more acutely in those places least responsible for emissions. The industrialised North does not have to contend with the full amount of wastes generated in the production of the goods they consume. Some wastes are exported, others are incurred in manufacturing operations in the industrialising South (where environmental regulation standards are generally more lax and resources and labour more cheaply priced), controlled by investors in the North. Finally, of course, many of the resources the wealthy consume come from the South, and therefore the impacts associated with resource depletion and extraction are borne by the people living in the areas where extraction takes place. The economic returns from the sale of these resources are insufficient to promote sustained economic growth, owing to undervalued terms of trade, but extraction continues apace to meet pressing debt requirements, creating a downward environment–poverty spiral.

Economic processes therefore affect a spatial outsourcing of environmental externalities. In this way, environmental degradation and insecurity can be seen to be a product of meta-processes of development in the industrialised North at the expense of underdevelopment in the industrialising South (for the original explanation of underdevelopment see Gunder Frank 1966). This book understands environmental insecurity to be the way the impacts of environmental degradation affect people in areas already subject to underdevelopment, where ecological problems exacerbate the social impact of economic processes affecting underdevelopment.

There is ample evidence pointing to increased environmental degradation and subsequent insecurity. When analysing such information the notion of biological (including human) and biophysical interdependence (ecology) must always be kept in mind. Focusing on any single problem limits appreciation of the broader processes and trends. Thus the Aristotelian observation that 'the sum of the parts does not equal the whole' (even assuming that we have a sum of parts) has its corresponding application in the understanding that 'the whole of the insecurity domain is greater than any of its parts' (Borrow 1996: 436). The following observations about environmental degradation and environmental insecurity should be seen, then, not only as problems in their own right, but also as signs indicating a far larger problem.

Environmental degradation

Environmental degradation is understood by this book to be the processes by which the life-sustaining functions of the biosphere are disturbed. So when this book refers to the problem of environmental degradation it is referring to the totality of a wide range of interdependent processes occurring at a range of scales and in different places to differing degrees. These processes include, among others, atmospheric pollution and climate change, biodiversity loss, soil loss, salinisation and acidification of soils and water, fisheries depletion, depletion of forests and timber, marine pollution, and contamination of plants and animals by synthetic chemicals and radioactive substances.

There are two aspects to the problem of environmental degradation. First, there are *sources* problems which arise when the supply of natural resources of direct use to humans decreases, and resource scarcities occur. This supply of materials problem is fundamental to Malthusian theories and was (perhaps mistakenly) the most popularly interpreted message of *The Limits to Growth* (Meadows *et al.* 1972). This aspect is as much economistic as it is ecological in that it concerns the scarcity of natural capital contributions to the economy. There is another, more complex aspect to the problem of environmental degradation which is the overloading of planetary *sinks* (McMichael 1993: 47). This refers to the accumulation of wastes emitted from dispersed sources and the biosphere's decreasing capacity to absorb these wastes, which accumulate in hydrological, soil and food cycles until both incremental and suddenly hazardous effects result (O'Riordan and Rayner 1991). These problems with sinks are arguably the more critical environmental issue, suggesting that there might be a threshold beyond which essential life support systems are no longer able to sustain certain forms of life – including our own. This is an *ecological* understanding of the problem of environmental degradation. There is, however, considerable overlap between the two aspects, whether we choose to emphasise sources or sinks.

Of all the human-induced environmental damage, most has occurred since 1950. It is thought that some 40 per cent of the earth's surface used to be covered with forests, whereas this figure is now 27 per cent and falling (Brown *et al.* 1996). One fifth of all tropical forests were lost in the thirty years 1960–1990 (Brown *et al.* 1998). This deforestation strongly implies declining biodiversity, although figures for this are difficult to produce as only 13 per cent of an estimated 13 million species have been scientifically described (UNEP 1997). Tropical rainforests cover only 7 per cent of the earth's surface yet contain an estimated 50 per cent of plant and animal species, so their decline has reduced biodiversity substantially. Every year some 20 million hectares of tropical rainforests are grossly degraded or completely destroyed (UNDP 1996). It is thought that up to fifty plant species become extinct every day (Seager 1995).

Coastal flora are also being cleared rapidly. In Latin America some 50 per cent of coastal mangroves are affected by forestry and aquaculture (UNEP 1997), and in Thailand aquaculture has destroyed 87 per cent of mangrove stands (Seager 1995). Degradation of coastal breeding habitats is a contributing factor to the depletion of many of the world's fisheries. Up to 60 per cent of the world's marine fisheries are now heavily exploited (UNEP 1997). In excess of three billion people rely in some manner on coastal and marine habitats for food and other needs, so it is disturbing that 34 per cent of the world's coastal regions are at high risk of degradation, with a further 17 per cent at moderate risk of degradation (UNDP 1998). Such degradation also results in heightened vulnerability to the effects of climate change.

Land degradation is an important component of the overall processes of environmental degradation. Deforestation, agriculture and overgrazing are the three principal causes. It is thought that some 20 per cent of Asia, 22 per cent of Africa and 25 per cent of Central America are affected (WRI 1992). The total area of land now degraded is nearly two billion hectares, with one billion people in 110 countries at risk from the impacts of the degradation of drylands (UNDP 1998, UNEP 1997). Land degradation contributes to decreased agricultural productivity. Africa in 1994 was producing 27 per cent less food than in 1967 (Seager 1995), and in 1995 the world grain harvest was less than world consumption (Brown *et al.* 1996). As the rate of population growth continues to outstrip the rate of increase in grain production, grain reserves are gradually diminishing (Brown *et al.* 1998).

Atmospheric pollutants are also a significant problem. All the world's major cities suffer from poor air quality (UNEP 1997). There is evidence to suggest that skin cancers are increasing in southern latitudes due to depletion of the stratospheric ozone layer (McMichael 1993). In 1997 worldwide carbon emissions reached an all-time high of 6.3 billion tons; 1997 was also the warmest year since records began to be kept 130 years ago, while the fourteen warmest years on record have occurred since 1979 (Brown *et al.* 1998). Scientific best estimates suggest this warming will cause increased climatic variability and a rise in average sea level (which has already risen by between 10 and 25 cm over the past hundred years) (IPCC 1995). Greater climatic variability is perhaps indicated by increased insurance claims for weather-related disasters, from $16 billion during the years 1980–90 to $48 billion during 1990–5 (Brown *et al.* 1996). Many insurance companies are incrementally reviewing policies that insure against the risk of weather-related losses.

Worldwide population numbers are increasing, as is the number of people living in urban areas. In 1995 the world's population increased by 80 million people, most of whom were born in industrialising countries (Brown *et al.* 1998). The world's population now stands at some six billion people, 1,200 times greater than it was at the time of the transition from hunter-gatherer to early farming societies around 10,000 years ago. Most of the growth in human numbers has occurred in the last 50 years. The overall rate of population growth is slowly declining, however, and in many areas population has already stabilised or is nearing zero growth.

Coupled with population growth has come a rise in the amount of extrasomatic (non-body) energy used per person, from approximately 1 Human Energy Equivalent (HEE) per person per day during the hunter-gatherer phase to today's level of 20 HEEs per person per day (after Boyden 1987, Boyden and Dovers 1997). If we take the use of extrasomatic energy as a rough guide, the total demand humans place on the biosphere has increased approximately 24,000 times from around 10,000 years ago.

Environmental insecurity

The problem of environmental insecurity is a more specific aspect of this broader problem of environmental degradation. Environmental insecurity is defined here as the vulnerability of people to the effects of environmental degradation. So environmental insecurity is more than the physical processes of environmental degradation; it includes the way this degradation affects the welfare of human beings. Environmental insecurity is therefore understood as a social problem, both for the way it impacts upon human welfare, and because the meta-problem of environmental degradation is a product of human behaviour.

Environmental insecurity is very much about risk. In the first instance a risk to biospheric integrity entails risks to human health. Some infectious diseases, including traditional diseases such as tuberculosis and malaria, have become more prevalent due to continued environmental degradation. Each year some 17 million people die from preventable curable diseases such as diarrhoea, malaria and measles, with diarrhoeal diseases affecting two billion people in the developing world, leading to the death of five million (three million of which are children) (UNDP 1998). In 1993 acute respiratory infections claimed 4.1 million lives. Further, in 1993 some 200 million people were thought to suffer from schistosomiasis, 4.3 million from whooping cough, and up to 500 million from malaria (Platt 1996). Water-borne diseases are still the largest cause of human illness and death worldwide, causing some 25,000 deaths per day (UNEP 1997). In 1997 the recorded number of HIV infections increased by 6 million, and in 1997 there were an estimated 2.3 million HIV-related deaths (Brown et al. 1998). Whilst there is much speculation about the origin of AIDS, it is generally considered that, like most infectious diseases, it arises because 'changes in human demography, culture and technological practice create ecological opportunities for microbes' (McMichael 1993: 282). The prevalence of many diseases is closely related to population density, poverty and malnutrition as well as environmental degradation. Of particular concern here is tuberculosis, once thought to have been nearly eradicated, but which is now carried by an estimated one third of the world's population (Harvard Working Group on New and Resurgent Diseases, 1996: 162). The 841 million people throughout the world who are malnourished are the most susceptible to infectious diseases (UNDP 1998).

Water scarcity and poor water quality are arguably the most important factors in environmental insecurity. It is estimated that by the year 2000 one quarter of the earth's land surface will face persistent water shortages, but already there are some 1.3 billion people who are without a reliable supply of safe water (UNEP 1997, UNDP 1998). It is thought that, if present trends continue, by 2050 there could be 1–2.5 billion people living in water-stressed areas. The problem of water scarcity and contamination is closely linked to that of land degradation.

It is human behaviour that contributes to the risk that the biosphere may be unable to sustain some life forms and some ways of living. The United Nations Conference on Environment and Development has joined the authors of *Our Common Future* in arguing that it is human insecurities such as poverty and inequality which are at the root of many environmental changes (WCED 1987, UNCED 1993). It is now conventional wisdom, therefore, that a range of seemingly unrelated human vulnerabilities cause environmental degradation and subsequent insecurity.

Poverty is an integral cause of vulnerability, and some 1.3 billion people presently live on less than US$1 per day, while nearly three billion people live on less that US$2 per day (UNDP 1998). The gap between the poor and the rich has steadily grown over the past 30 years: by 1996 'the gap in per capita income between the industrial and developing worlds tripled, from US$5,700 in 1960 to US$15,400 in 1993' (UNDP 1996: 2). Indeed, so great is the disparity that the combined wealth of the 225 richest people in the world is equal to the annual income of the poorest 47 per cent of the world's population (UNDP 1998: 30).

Women and children are particularly vulnerable. Worldwide, half a million women die each year from causes related to childbirth, and in 1990 in the least developed countries the average maternal mortality rate was 1,100 deaths per 100,000 live births, as opposed to 30 deaths per 100,000 in industrial countries (UNDP 1998). In industrialised countries the wage rate for women is two thirds that for men (UNDP 1996). Children are no more secure than females, and female children are more vulnerable than male children. In India and China, for example, infant females are far more likely to die than infant males (suggesting that it is extremely difficult to disengage population reduction programmes from violence) (Brown *et al.* 1996). More than 12 million children under the age of five die each year, mostly due to malnutrition, and 30 per cent of all children under five in industrialising countries are underweight (UNDP 1998).

Militarisation is arguably the single biggest institutional risk to human beings. The effects of militarisation come not merely from warfare, but also from the preparation for warfare and the opportunity costs to society foreclosed by military expenditure. It is estimated that up to 90 per cent of casualties from conflicts in the 1990s were civilians, with at least three million killed during armed conflict in the first half of the 1990s (Brown et al. 1998). In conflict zones throughout the world there are in excess of 100 million people who are chronically malnourished (UNDP 1996). By 1995 there were some 100 million landmines lying in the soils of 64 countries – an indiscriminate threat to the health and welfare of large numbers of people throughout the world (Brown et al. 1996).

That militarisation continues to generate insecurity is made possible by the levels of expenditure on the military-industrial complex. Governments pay out large sums to buy 'security' of one kind at the expense of security of other kinds. An estimated US$8 trillion (US$8 million million) has been spent on nuclear weapons alone since 1945 (Sivard 1996). Worldwide, an average of 2.9 per cent of every nation's Gross Domestic Product (GDP) was spent on defence in 1996 (UNDP 1998). There are vast discrepancies, however: US military spending remained in excess of US$260 billion per annum; the Russian Federation spent US$69 billion; France US$46 billion; Australia US$8 billion; Myanmar US$1.9 billion; New Zealand US$729 million; Bangladesh US$517 million; and Guyana US$7 million (UNDP 1998).

Certain forms of insecurity are being lessened. The world's stockpile of nuclear weapons, long perceived as the single biggest threat to human survival, is gradually decreasing. Globally, the levels of military expenditure have been on a downward trend since 1987 (Sivard 1996). There are positive signs on some health issues: smallpox has recently been completely eradicated, and polio has been eliminated in 145 countries (Brown et al. 1996). Between 1960 and 1993 average life expectancy in industrialising countries increased from 46 to 62 years; the average infant mortality rate fell by more than half; the under 5 years old mortality rate fell by more than half; and now 80 per cent of people in industrialising countries have access to basic health services and 70 per cent have access to safe water (UNDP 1996). Females are increasingly attaining higher levels of education (UNDP 1998).

Consumption and redistribution are key concepts for understanding environmental insecurity. Consumption of energy, food and other resources is much higher in industrialised countries, and so a far larger amount of wastes is generated. Overconsumption in industrialised countries is therefore the primary cause of resource depletion and the overloading of planetary sinks. According to the United Nations Development Programme (UNDP), the average person in a developed country produces as much pollution and consumes as many resources as 30–50 people in the developing world (UNDP 1998). The population of the developing countries is four times greater than that of developed countries, yet those in developing countries produce only 37.4 per cent of all carbon dioxide emissions (UNDP 1998). The per capita consumption of commercial energy in 1994 was eight times greater in the developed world than in the developing world, but the principal source of energy in developing countries, firewood, is becoming more scarce (UNDP 1998). It is estimated that by the year 2000 over 2.9 billion people will face firewood shortages, an increase of 1.2 billion people since 1980 (Seager 1995). A contributing factor in deforestation is paper consumption; in North America each person consumed an average of 302 kg of paper in 1991, whereas in Africa the average person consumed only 6 kg of paper in the same year (Seager 1995).

This overconsumption and lack of redistribution produces a double insecurity whereby longstanding vulnerabilities arising from underdevelopment and impoverishment are compounded by an intensifying suite of risks associated with environmental degradation. For example, a Bangladeshi person has a life expectancy twenty-one years less than a resident of Australia; a Bangladeshi woman is ninety times more likely to die when giving birth than a woman from Australia; and an average person from Australia consumes 90 times more commercial energy than a person from Bangladesh (UNDP 1998). There are therefore clear inequities and injustices between these two countries, environmental insecurities aside. To compound this, however, an average Australian produces eighty times more greenhouse gases than the average person in Bangladesh (greatly increasing the Australian's responsibility for environmental insecurity), yet within 50 years up to 18 per cent of Bangladesh could be flooded by sea-level rises, whereas a much smaller amount of Australia's surface is likely to go under. Furthermore, Australia has much greater wealth as a nation (Australia's Gross Domestic Product in 1993 was 12 times greater than that of Bangladesh), as do its individual residents (GDP/capita is 14 times greater), giving it a relatively much greater capacity to adapt to sea-level rise and increased climatic variability (UNDP 1996). The difference is that while for an Australian environmental insecurity is a problem of adaptation, for a Bangladeshi it is a matter of life and death. There are therefore discrepancies in responsibility for and vulnerability to environmental problems. For those in underdeveloped areas, environmental degradation is increasingly creating a double vulnerability referred to here as 'environmental insecurity'.

The defence of environmental insecurity

The continued non-resolution of environmental insecurity motivates this book. Despite growing awareness of environmental changes, and long-standing awareness of material insecurities, the problems persist. There can be little doubt that the world is aware of famine and malnutrition in Africa, clearfelling of rainforests in Central America, the continued abuse of women and children, and the real possibility of sea-level rises. Why these problems have not been resolved is a vexed question. In part, answering this question requires explorations of, and conversations about, impediments to change and the reforms necessary to enable change. This book hopes to make some contribution in these areas.

There is a tendency to assume that there is a will for reform to overcome environmental problems and by implication environmental insecurity, and that the impediments are matters of structure and attitude. The history of world development since the fifteenth century, however, has been one of exploitation of the South for the material betterment of the North, and the maintenance and defence of this relationship largely through military means (conquest), administrative means (colonisation), and now additionally through investment (economic globalisation). These contemporary trading patterns, whereby wealth is returned to the North and the environmental externalities are borne by the South, leaves the Northern countries generally free from severe problems such as water contamination, toxification of food, land degradation and energy shortages. The problems they do incur are often treatable by technological means afforded by relatively great private and public resources. In terms of global environmental problems such as climate change, better infrastructure, greater personal mobility, private capital, a well-developed insurance industry and well-financed and strong state institutions render the North more resilient. These resilience-enhancing capacities are all underwritten by patterns of trade and investment which expand the material, financial and ecological footprint of Northern countries across a space far greater than their own borders. Conversely, the underdeveloped countries' material, financial and ecological footprint is limited to a space less than their own borders, and hence they are unable to maximise even the resources within their own domain to assist in their adaptation to environmental changes.

We might expect, then, that as environmental pressures mount, particularly those of a global nature which may affect developed countries (such as climate change), existing patterns of development and underdevelopment that favour the already powerful may be strengthened, or at least obstinately maintained, as these provide the means to ensure resilience and ease the problems of adaptation. Thus the processes that create environmental insecurity may be defended so that the relatively secure remain so. Many Northern writings and policy pronouncements on environmental security are discursive primers for exactly this kind of defence of the environmental security of the North at the expense of the environmental insecurity of the majority of the world's population. The means of this defence include the traditional response of the deployment of military power.

3

Security
From What and for Whom?

The concept of environmental security stems mainly from an understanding of security, and more particularly national security, developed within the discipline of international relations. To appreciate the genesis and meaning of environmental security, this is where one needs to begin. The concept of security also warrants exploration because it distinguishes environmental security from other environmental problem-solving concepts such as sustainable development.

The concept of security

Security is a universal yet nebulous concept which, despite lying at the heart of contemporary political theory, has generally been under-theorised (Buzan 1991). The word comes from the Latin *securitas*, meaning 'lack of care' (Dower 1995). According to the *Shorter Oxford Dictionary*, security is: '1. the condition of being protected from or not exposed to danger; safety. 2. freedom from doubt. Now chiefly, well founded confidence, certainty. 3. Freedom from care, anxiety or apprehension; a feeling of safety' (Little *et al*. 1973: 1927). The use of 'secure' as an adjective is dated to 1533 and its use as a verb is dated to 1593, the latter being defined as: '1. To make free from care or apprehension ... b. to satisfy, convince. Also to make (a person) feel secure of or against some contingency' (Little *et al.*, 1973: 1926). Historically, then, the concept of security has been concerned with safety, certainty and, by implication, maintenance of the status quo.

Security is something intuitively desirable. It can be characterised in two ways. First, it can be subject-specific, entailing stability in the face of

23

a particular risk. The particular risk can be referred to as the *what* of security. The risk of food shortages is an example of an answer to this *what* question. Second, security can be more generically understood as an entity in its own right, that is as a state of low risk and (relative) stability of all things to a given person or community. In both cases there is a particular object or group to be secured (Dower 1995). The particular entity to be secured can be referred to as the *who*, or referent, of security. In the case of the uncertainty of food availability, the *who* to be secured is the group at risk from food shortages. As a minimum standard, both the *who* and the *what* questions ought to be satisfied in any consistent discussion of security. Further, in as much as contemporary understandings of security talk in terms of threats and dangers, it is often revealing to ask *where* is the threat perceived to come from and *how*? Other questions that might be asked in order to clarify an account of security are: *how much security? By what means? At what cost?* And *in what time period*? (Baldwin 1997). These questions constitute a framework for the interrogation of security theories and policies.

The concept of security is inherently about risk and vulnerability. Risk is an inescapably subjective assessment. There is no purely objective basis upon which to assess the probability of food shortages, military aggression, a nuclear reactor accident, or rape. We can say, on the basis of evidence, that such events might in a general sense be more or less likely, and we can consider with some accuracy the impact of such an event, but we cannot objectively quantify the risk *per se*. The assessment of risk and security is therefore a subjective and value-laden process; for this reason, a judgement made by an expert on behalf of others should be open to debate. The availability and character of information and knowledge therefore become important components of security risk assessment. It follows that expert assessments of risk and security are suspect when the information that informs them is not freely available.

In this sense there is no 'reality' to risk and security. This makes it possible for people to feel secure despite a seemingly high degree of risk and, conversely, to feel insecure yet be relatively free from risk (Dower 1995). For example, environmental degradation is – and may increasingly be – a significant risk to the welfare of people, yet the degree to which this is perceived by most people is questionable. Alternatively, the likelihood of military aggression against a country such as Australia is (at least implicitly) considered by policy makers to be high (hence billions spent on defence), yet the likelihood that Australia will be invaded is arguably extremely low. The meaning of security is therefore ambiguous and contested, despite its relatively unchanging praxis (Buzan 1991).

Security is a power word, a 'speech act' that operationalises state monopolisation of responses to a challenge once it is labelled a security issue (Waever 1995: 55). Interpreting a challenge as a security problem raises its status: it is no longer merely a problem to be dealt with through mainstream institutions, but instead requires extraordinary measures. In the same way that the US is now engaged in a 'war on drugs', suggesting a response of a kind equivalent to war, labelling a particular challenge a security issue scripts that challenge as a threat to sovereignty, consequently excusing the state from the normal checks on its behaviour. This is a critically important aspect of the use of security; it raises the stakes of certain problems and justifies drastic and potentially unaccountable action. This is what is meant by 'securitisation', and it is an important and underlying theme of the politics of security and environmental security.

A (very) brief history of national security

The origins of national security can be traced to the principalities of Europe in the Renaissance. Warfare among the principalities was common and was initiated by expansionism, requiring in turn defence of one's own territory. The ruling elite synergised their external ambitions with their internal constituents through an informal contract whereby protection was offered in exchange for revenues and labour to fight wars (Lipschutz 1992a). It was during this period that one of the earliest (nominally) realist texts, Machiavelli's *The Prince*, was written (1513). The concept of security that emerged during this period was strongly equated with territorial defence. As with contemporary security discourse, however, behind the geopolitical rationale lies the real referent to be secured: not so much the delimited space *per se*, but rather the ruling security makers, who draw their power from the control of that space. National security, then, is a particularly if no longer exclusively European concept, and is integrally associated with the maintenance of elite power.

Up until the mid-seventeenth century the authority of the European city-states was undermined by the authority of the church, to the extent that the church could dictate where and when fighting could take place (Boulding 1992). In 1648, at the end of the Thirty Years' War, the states of Europe negotiated the Treaty of Westphalia which began the demise of the church as the highest authority and ushered in the age of sovereign political communities. National security is a consequence of the emergence of the territorially defined and militarily capable sovereign state as a law unto its own. Indeed, it can be argued that security is 'the constitutive principle' of the modern nation-state (Paggi and Pinzauti 1985: 8). National security is thus the product of particular, relatively recent historical circumstances; it is neither a timeless nor a universal truth.

After Westphalia, states engaged in a system of cooperation and conflict with few formal rules to guide behaviour. This system of relations between sovereign domains spread as the European powers expanded their claims to their colonies, and consolidated their control of these places. By the beginning of the First World War in 1914, nearly all the land surface of the earth was divided into political divisions, although few of these places were independent.

The classical political realist theory of security emerged after the Second World War. Between the world wars the approach to security was one which emphasised democracy, arbitration, disarmament and collective security (Baldwin 1997). The post-1945 theoretical orthodoxy defined itself against the failure of the inter-war period – particularly the policies of British Prime Minister Neville Chamberlain – to prevent the outbreak of war. This resurgent realism recentred security in the autonomy of the nation-state and emphasised the use of force as a means to resolve conflict between states (Baldwin 1997). A number of works were written which outlined the realist approach to security. An important forerunner was Carr's *The Twenty Years Crisis* (1939), but the most frequently cited 'great text' of realism is Morgenthau's *Politics Among Nations* (1950). Morgenthau considered that the security of the state was best achieved by the maximisation of military power which in turn depended on national economic scale and territorial size, national self-sufficiency in resources, and strong technological capability (Morgenthau 1950). Throughout much of the Cold War, and arguably beyond, this realist security theory held sway over policy makers. Brief mention must be made of neo-realism, a modified version of classical realism commonly identified as beginning with Waltz's *Man, the State and War* (1959). Both neo-realism and classical realism are state-centric and have a foundational belief in anarchy, and the distinction is not overly important to the purpose of this book.

National security and strategy

With the advent of the Cold War, security studies were increasingly conflated with strategic studies, particularly in the United States. The suite of ambiguities associated with national security were reduced to the technicalities of military, particularly nuclear, strategy. This reduction of security to strategy obscures and deflects attention from the presumed value of security itself by rendering it less substantial than the hard reality of weaponry (Dyer 1996: 30). By writing the world as one full of armed enemies, strategic discourse renders 'organised peacelessness' the normal condition (Klein 1989: 102).

Throughout the Cold War the national security theoretical orthodoxy (and practice) was premised upon a view of the state as a unitary and rational political actor who (following a simple abstraction that conflates polity with personality) behaves similarly to the way individual people are thought to behave. This model of human nature, informing the realist understanding of state behaviour, is based on idealised masculine traits of (instrumental) rationality, power seeking, competition, independence and autonomy (Tickner 1992). In this respect the compatriot of the *Homo economicus* of neoliberal economic theory is the *Homo securitas* of realist theory.

Security theory after the start of the Cold War viewed the international arena as having few rules or norms to guide behaviour; it saw the state's ability to use force to be both the principal threat and principal means to national security. This belief in the utility of power transferred directly into US policy, as evident in the landmark 1950 *NSC 68: United States Objectives and Programs for National Security* report, which argued that:

> It was and continues to be cardinal in this policy that we possess superior overall power in ourselves or in dependable combination with other like-minded nations. One of the most important ingredients of power is military strength. In the concept of 'containment' the maintenance of a strong military posture is deemd to be essential for two reasons: (1) as an ultimate guarantee of our national security and (2) as an indispensable backdrop to the conduct of the policy of 'containment'. Without superior aggregate military strength, in being and readily mobilizable, a policy of 'containment' – which is in effect a policy of calculated and gradual coercion – is no more than a policy bluff. (*NSC 68*, reprinted in May 1993: 41)

The extent to which this political realist theory of security still influences policy is the subject of considerable debate, with many arguing that idealist and liberal theories are increasingly influential. A more nuanced understanding is that the simple theoretical opposition or 'great debate' between realism and its counterparts of idealism and liberalism serves as a 'substitute for serious theoretical reflection and critical engagement' about the state of world politics (Walker 1993: 107). As this book's analysis of US environmental security policy aims to show, realism still has considerable influence on security discourse and policy. This is particularly evident in the 'fortress' response of many industrialised states to what they perceive to be a world disorder likened to a 'jungle full of snakes' (Sachs 1995, Rogers 1994). In short, despite increased interdependence, changes in the global economy and a proliferation of 'new' security concerns, the state is still fundamentally self-serving and holds fast to its sovereignty, with security as its constitutive principle. Indeed it is a reasonable hypothesis that the reinterpretation of security to include new threats (see Chapter 4) is the discursive regeneration of this constitutive principle in a post-Cold War era where wars are more often domestic than international, and where violence (direct and structural) is increasingly the product of Northern economic hegemony rather than interstate rivalry.

So, although the meaning and effect of realism can be overdetermined, Campbell's contention that realism is 'the most common metatheoretical discourse among practitioners of the discipline of International Relations' still holds true (Campbell 1992: 4). Traces of realism can be found in contemporary security policies; take the 1998 *US National Security Strategy*, for example:

> The US military plays an essential role in building coalitions and shaping the international environment in ways that protect and promote US interests. Through overseas presence and peacetime engagement activities such as defense cooperation, security assistance, and training and exercises with allies and friends, our armed forces help to deter aggression and coercion, promote regional stability, prevent and reduce conflicts and threats, and serve as role models for militaries in emerging democracies.... Our nuclear deterrent posture is one of the most visible and important examples of how US military capabilities can be used effectively to deter aggression and coercion, as reaffirmed in a Presidential Decision Directive signed by President Clinton in November 1997. Nuclear weapons serve as a hedge against an uncertain

future, a guarantee of our security commitments to allies and a disincentive to those who would contemplate developing or otherwise acquiring their own nuclear weapons. (Clinton 1998: 12)

This equation of military capability with power in international affairs is a hallmark of realist theory and policy, and is also evident in the Australian 1994 Defence White Paper:

Maintaining a defence force capable of ensuring that armed force is not suc-cessfully used against Australia is essential because armed force remains a factor in international affairs. It continues to be one of the ways in which national power can be asserted and national self-interest pursued. (Commonwealth of Australia 1994: 3)

A cogent definition of security from the realist perspective is difficult. Clements is perhaps closest to the mark in saying that security is 'whatever national security elites say it is', suggesting that security is a vehicle for the exercise of power over domestic society (1990: 3). Nevertheless, in general the 'who' of the realist understanding of security is the nation-state, the 'what' is most frequently war, and the source of the threat is other groups of people. For realists, peace is seen as a contractual matter rather than as a moral obligation. In this view, peace means the absence of direct violence (notably war), and this is at best a temporary abeyance of the inevitable recurrence of conflict. Thus in realist theory 'peace is, by definition, an armed peace' (Paggi and Pinzauti 1985: 6).

The prevailing approach to national security understands the state as a given rather than as a socially constructed and therefore mutable entity. Indeed, for all the emphasis placed on the integrity of nation-state, there is a general absence of theorisation about the state itself (Walker 1993). This view of the nation-state as a coherent, natural and preordained entity excludes the historicist understanding of the state as a particular product of recent history. So, with the realist approach to security, world politics is 'portrayed as a permanent game, which can appear to have followed the same rules more or less since time immemorial' (Walker 1995: 321). In this respect realism is conservative, its commitment to the world *as it is* forecloses on the possibility of change, and instead it reasserts (continually) the impossibility of lasting peace (Linklater 1995).

A narrow reading of history also explains realism's bad faith model of human nature. This approach not only reduces the history of politics to an ahistoric nation-state, it also denies alternative readings of history which in turn 'reduces the possibility of politics, by erecting the spectre of the permanent adversary, against which perpetual vigilance is needed' (Dalby 1990a: 158). As Gandhi reminds us, however, history is a ledger of rare instances of violence rather than a record of more commonplace instances of cooperation (Gandhi 1951).

The reality of the world in which national security is seen to be necessary is open to differing interpretations. This makes expensive and dangerous security policies based on a questionable reality at best an unnecessary use of resources, and at worst a perpetuation of mutual perceptions of threat, requiring the acquisition of ever more powerful weaponry, thereby generating more insecurity and triggering arms races. This is what is known as the 'security dilemma'. Realism sees the security dilemma as inevitable, making the expertise of security strategists indispensable for a nation to successfully negotiate world politics. From a critical perspective, however, the security dilemma is the (not inevitable) product of one particular representation of world politics. It would have far less relevance were not national security premised on the construction of the world as an anarchic and brutal place. The security dilemma neatly highlights the unreason in national security rationality.

National security discourse is engaged in the identification of Others who threaten the cohesion and purpose of the state. There are two principal functions of this construction of Others. First, while these Others principally lie outside the nation–state, the possibility that they might also reside within helps to justify surveillance and control of political activity within the state (Dalby 1990b: 172). Throughout the Cold War the states aligned with both the Soviet Union and the United States monitored and persecuted domestic individuals and groups which held different political values. In the US the repression of socialist and communist movements was seen to be justified on the grounds that these groups were unpatriotic and a threat to national security. The real threat posed by these groups was the possibility that they might undermine the legitimacy of the state and its elite. So national security discourse *secures itself* from debate and democratic participation by invoking the supposed necessity for secrecy, and by setting standards of behaviour that make challenging the wisdom of national security an unpatriotic act.

The second function of the Other is to construct a sense of the nation which is determined solely in terms of how that nation differs from Others. National security discourse is a key part of the way the state universalises identity and seeks to control difference; it therefore helps to secure the common identity necessary for the 'nation' in the nation-state. A national identity can only be sustained if applied universally, making nationalism inherently intolerant and denigrative of different groups in different places. As it depicts the outside world as full of dangerous Others, mainstream national security discourse marginalises consideration of domestic sources of insecurity. Violences such as rape, disappearances and unlawful imprisonment are scripted as subordinate insecurities to the meta-insecurity of warfare. This helps to ignore the many ways in which the state is a principal source of insecurity (actively or complicitly by its inaction).

The efficacy of national security is premised on the ability to control space. According to Gray, for example, 'the influence of the geographical setting upon international power relations' is so pervasive that 'there can be no ... escape from the struggle for power' (Gray 1996: 259 and 254). There is thus a 'practical geopolitical reasoning' which underwrites orthodox national security and strategy (O'Tuathail and Agnew 1992). In this geographically imagined account of the world the complex geographies of global ecological, economic, cultural and political processes are all reduced into a simplistic dualism between inside and outside. These complementary inside/outside and Us/Other dichotomies truncate meaningful examination of the links between the causes and effects of insecurity. The responsibility for threat – and the necessity to organise society to meet it – is attributed to the distanced Other on the outside; in this way 'our complicity in evil is erased' (Campbell 1993: 3). Thus the mutual nature of the security dilemma is suppressed; Klein calls this a 'textual strategy to mask responsibility' (1989: 104). So in thinking critically about insecurity it becomes clear that the enemy is also Us (Walker 1988, Dalby 1998a).

The construction of Us (the nation) through discourses of Otherness involves the fostering of domestic economic mobilisation because 'the Enemy stimulates growth and initiative ... by virtue of the fact that the whole of society becomes a defense society' (Marcuse 1964: 51). More broadly, the notion of security has been integral to the generation of Western political/economic hegemony in the post-Second World War era, as clearly demonstrated in *NSC 68*'s reference to the Marshall Plan:

> United States foreign economic policy has been designed to assist in the building of such a system and such conditions in the free world. The principal

features of this policy can be summarized as follows: ... 3) assistance in the development of underdeveloped areas; ... 7) efforts to reestablish an international economy based on multilateral trade, declining trade barriers, and convertible currencies (the GATT–ITO program, the Reciprocal Trade Agreements program, the IMF–IBRD program....) In both their short and long term aspects, these policies and programs are directed to the strengthening of the free world and therefore to the frustration of the Kremlin design. (NSC 68, reprinted in May 1993: 48)

Thus security was the 'mechanism for binding the civil societies of the West and its aspiring allies' as liberal societies sought to construct a global order that conformed to Western norms (Klein 1997: 362). Security as a cultural practice that defends the common (liberal) way of life cannot therefore be separated from development in the post-war period. This strong association of national security with post-war development, and more generally with the foundation of the modern nation-state, makes national security an integral part of the history of ecological and social damage.

Mainstream discourses of national security normalise danger, threat and risk. The risk seen to be most important is that of the (eternal) danger of armed aggression from outside. It sees this risk as natural, implying that violence is a natural aspect of human nature and political behaviour. This particular discourse of risk is like all discourses of risk in that it is socially constructed. It is therefore contestable and, more than most, deserves serious attention for its expensive habits and destructive effects. When risk is narrowly interpreted in this way strategies for resilience are dominated by strategic planning to deter and engage with armed forces. In this sense the response of national security to uncertainty is negative and reactive. It presents immediate 'solutions' that are really exacerbations of insecurity and uncertainty.

As this book will show, much contemporary writing on environmental security, and virtually all policy statements on the subject, flow from this prevailing, nominally realist approach to security. This is a fundamental source of the paradoxes and politics of environmental security. The following chapter will explore in depth the literature which, in seeking to 'redefine security', introduced environmental considerations into mainstream security discourse. This served to broaden the array of responses to the question security from what? beyond military threats to encompass economic, energy, food and environmental issues.

4

New Security Issues
The Old Guard Looks for New Targets

From the 1970s onwards, a period which coincided with detente between the superpowers and the integration of critical theory into the social sciences, an array of writings have set out to provide alternative answers to the question: *security from what?* Different types of risks to national security have been identified under a common understanding that 'new threats are emerging, threats with which military forces cannot cope' (Brown 1977: 5). This identification of new security issues received further impetus with the fall of the Berlin Wall. A suite of pre-existing 'dangers' (mostly to US interests) were re-emphasised, such as the strength of the Japanese and German economies (economic security), global environmental change (environmental security), an array of difficulties associated with the 'Third World', and energy availability (energy security). Other security issues which are now identified include drug trafficking (the 'war on drugs'), failed states which may behave aggressively inwardly and outwardly, transboundary crime, hostage taking, terrorism, ethno-political conflicts, the migration of diseases and people across national borders, and the (existential) threat posed by large groups of people who subscribe to a different religious orientation than that of the Judaeo-Christian West (Islam gets much attention) (after Campbell 1992, Dalby 1997). To this list we can add concerns over food security. In as much as politics in the post-Cold War era has changed, the addition of new threats to the security agenda is to a large degree the product of old orders looking for new rationales for their existence.

In his influential book *People, States and Fear* Buzan identifies five major sectors or components of national security: military security, political security, societal security, economic security, and ecological security

(Buzan 1991). For Buzan, political security is about 'the organisational stability of states, systems of government and the ideologies that give them legitimacy', while societal security 'concerns the sustainability, within acceptable conditions for evolution, of traditional patterns of language, culture and religious national identity and custom' (1991: 19). Buzan's definition of political security pertains to the maintenance of the requisite conditions for nationalism and national resilience, and as such is an explicit statement of the implicit function of mainstream security discourse. The concept of societal security has little utility, and were it taken seriously would in all likelihood lead not to the protection of (definitionally ambiguous) culture within the (undefinable) limits of evolution, but rather to the fortification and calcification of particular stereotypes at the expense of everyday lived culture. In so far as this societal security also concerns national identity, again we see the presumption of the nation, revealing, as others have suggested, the extent to which Buzan's analysis occurs within the context of realism even as it seeks to move beyond it (Shaw 1993).

Energy security

Energy use has increased massively since the onset of the industrial revolution, and particularly in the post-Second World War period. This expansion received a severe setback in 1973 when the Organisation of Petroleum Exporting Countries (OPEC) quadrupled the price of oil on world markets, creating considerable anxiety for both industrialised and industrialising economies alike. By constricting temporarily the lifeblood of industrial economies (energy), the oil crisis demonstrated the vulnerability of national economies to the dictates of the global economy: 'for the US public, the lines at the gas pumps which the OPEC crisis produced forced a rapid understanding of our economic and energy interdependence' (Stephenson 1988: 62). The current notion of energy security stems from this period (although it has earlier manifestations, for example much of the naval conflict in the Pacific during the Second World War was driven by the need to secure/disrupt sea lanes for delivery of energy resources).

Energy security is the theory and practice of securing energy for the nation-state. According to a recent report by the Trilateral Commission (North America, Western Europe and Japan), energy security is maintained by utilising national power to secure a steady supply of affordable energy (read 'oil') for the purposes of economic growth (Martin *et al.* 1996). The continued importance of oil supply is made clear in this report: the Gulf War is referred to as the 'successful defense of Kuwait and Saudi Arabia' and is seen to be demonstrative of the understanding that 'energy security requires foresight and years of preparation' (Martin *et al.* 1996: 16). Such accounts of energy security are common, they countenance the projection of force to secure uninterrupted supplies of oil, and the pragmatic and at times forceful engagement with nations who by dint of (mis)fortune have energy resources but apparently little sovereignty. The 1990–1 US National Security Strategy was unselfconscious about this:

> Secure supplies of energy are essential to our prosperity and security. The concentration of 65 percent of the world's known oil reserves in the Persian Gulf means we must continue to ensure reliable access to competitively priced oil and a prompt, adequate response to any major oil supply disruption. (Bush 1990: 83)

The problem of energy security is not only the need to alleviate scarcity, however, but also concerns the ecological impact of burning fossil fuels. The only presently viable solution is clean renewable energy technologies such as solar and wind power, or abstinence and greater efficiency of energy use. The impediments to these alternatives are less technical and economic, but rather political (Dovers 1994).

Economic security

The oil embargo accelerated examination of the economic dimensions of national security. This gave rise to the term economic security, which implies regular access to those resources, finance and markets necessary to sustain national economic growth and state power. As suggested in the previous chapter, economic and military concerns have been inseparable in post-war United States security policy. In more recent times US security policy makes more explicit reference to the importance of protecting access to those materials, markets and investments necessary for US economic growth and military power:

> Our economic and security interests are inextricably linked. Prosperity at home depends on stability in key regions with which we trade or from which we import critical commodities, such as oil and natural gas. Prosperity also

demands our leadership in international development, financial and trade institutions. In turn, the strength of our diplomacy, our ability to maintain an unrivalled military and the attractiveness of our values abroad depend in large part on the strength of our economy. (Clinton 1998: 31)

Economic security is associated with the export of capitalist values: consumption becomes the standard of the good life, and Western producers become its suppliers (Barnet 1984). For the US at least, economic security is thus a discourse of economic self-interest justifying muted imperialist foreign policies to preserve national economic power. As the above quotation from the 1998 National Security Strategy suggests, economic security is inseparable from national security not simply because economically unfavourable conditions jeopardise the national interest, but because economic power is a crucial determinant of military power, and because the state at times uses its military power to advance its economic agenda.

Food security

At the same time as the oil embargo (1973), the US grain stockpile and cropland reserve failed (for the first time) to hedge against global food shortages (taking into account distortions in distribution), and the concept of food security became a practical concern (Brown 1977). Like the oil crisis, the impending food shortages highlighted the vulnerability of those countries which depended on outside sources for food. Food security has been understood primarily in terms of national resilience, as 'a common source of political instability' (Brown 1977: 7). Thus the notion has largely remained captured by discourses of national security. In a more intuitive sense, however, food security introduced a dimension to security that could not be completely fixed to the nation-state. Couched in terms of Maslow's hierarchy of needs, food (and water) security pertains as much to the basic right of people to fundamental subsistence requirements (Maslow 1954). Later understandings of food security have broken away from the statist perspective; for example, the UNDP defines food security as the right of all people to physical and economic access to basic food (UNDP 1994). This understanding of food security (for people) is closely related to that of environmental security for people: 'for rural producers in developing countries, the distinction between food insecurity and the environment does not exist' (Davies et al. 1991: 19).

The environment as a security issue

Environmental degradation has been a central issue in the reinterpretation and redefinition of security. Richard Falk's *This Endangered Planet* (1971) is a landmark in the literature that links environmental issues to security. Falk did not coin the phrase environmental security, but he established many themes still central to the concept. Falk describes the relationship between resource scarcity and violence as being one of the mobilisation of the already powerful to defend against those who have less power:

> [U]nder world conditions of insufficient resources to satisfy total demand there is a natural tendency for those with less to seek a larger share. This tendency induces those with a larger share to organise their defences against those with less and to use their superiority to obtain still more. The rich get richer, the powerful grow more so. (Falk 1971: 59)

So, for Falk, the powerful are likely to deploy the means of violence to maintain their power in the face of increasing calls for justice. The implication is that responsibility for violent behaviour, and conversely for finding peaceful solutions, rests primarily with the already wealthy and powerful.

Falk is not immune to the idea that engendering a sense of urgency about environmental problems is necessary to induce change. He is sensitive, however, to the presentation of problems in the language of crisis, arguing that 'the great danger of an apocalyptic argument is that to the extent that it persuades, it also immobilizes' (1971: 5). This is an observation of relevance for the notion of environmental security, which has a tendency to present environmental problems in apocalyptic tones. This approach does little to stimulate constructive and positive engagement with the substantive problems, particularly their causes. A question emerges, then, about the politics of discourse. This pre-empts the larger debate, discussed later, about whether addressing environmental problems in terms of security is a desirable strategy.

Another early publication that explores the links between environmental degradation and security is Brown's *Redefining National Security* (1977). Although the title suggests that Brown remains captured by the 'national' component of security, an underlying intent of the paper is to problematise national security practices:

In a world that is not only ecologically interdependent but economically and politically interdependent as well, the concept of 'national' security is no longer adequate.... Neither individual security nor national security can be sensibly considered in isolation. In effect, the traditional military concept of 'national security' is growing ever less adequate. (Brown 1977: 40–1)

Brown specifically addresses the deterioration of biophysical systems and identifies four systems under stress: fisheries, grasslands, forests and croplands. He also discusses the problem of climate modification, and all his concerns relate to food security. Brown considers that militaries are incapable of meeting the challenges posed to human well-being by the deterioration of biophysical systems: 'National defense establishments are useless against these new threats. Neither bloated military budgets nor highly sophisticated weapons systems can halt deforestation or solve the firewood crisis now affecting so many Third World countries' (Brown 1977: 37). Brown therefore makes the reasonable suggestion that disarmament and budgetary reallocations are important initiatives for resolving environmental degradation. *Redefining National Security*'s main contribution is a cogent overview of the social processes that pressure biophysical systems, their physical responses, and the resulting implications for human welfare. It should have provided policy makers and security analysts with an excellent background to the ecological dimensions of security, and its implications should have led to a set of responses that took these causes and effects seriously. Yet subsequent literature and policy rarely demonstrate the same degree of awareness.

In 1983 Ullman's 'Redefining Security' was published. The principal contribution of this widely cited paper is the definition of a national security threat as anything which can quickly degrade the quality of life of the inhabitants of a state, or which narrows the choices available to people and organisations within the state. 'Redefining Security' is notable for its crude discussion of Third World poverty as an engine for armed conflict and illegal immigration, suggesting that environmental degradation is 'likely to make Third World governments more militarily confrontational in their relations with the advanced, industrialised nations' (Ullman 1983: 142). Ullman's imagery is provocative: 'the image of islands of affluence amidst a sea of poverty is not an inaccurate one', and 'the pressure engendered by population growth in the Third World is bound to degrade the quality of life, and diminish the range of options available, to governments and persons in the rich countries' (Ullman 1983: 143).

This reference to islands of affluence may become accurate only in so far as this imagery contributes to a defensive Western disposition which reifies the theory. Further, the assumption that deprived 'Third World governments' may be 'more militarily confrontational' is notable. The possibility that they might seek to resist and engage for their betterment through non-violent means is not countenanced.

Ullman argues that 'conflict over resources is likely to grow more intense' (Ullman 1983: 139). Lost in the analysis, however, is consideration of *who* will initiate this conflict. As Falk suggests, it may not be the poor who resort to force of arms (see above). Ullman is concerned with *national* security and threats to US interests. These are identified as coming from outside the nation-state in the form of disrupted access to essential resources, and proxy wars. To the list of traditional threats Ullman also adds the possibility of illegal immigration by environmental refugees (now a popular concern). Thus Ullman views the South's environmental insecurity as a problem only in as much as it potentially endangers the quality of life for the governments and inhabitants of the North. Little concern is paid to the problems that are experienced in these Other places, problems which are surely of concern in and of themselves. These early analytical closures have been rewritten subsequently throughout much of the environmental security literature. In many ways Ullman's paper stands at the watershed of contemporary environmental security studies. It carries with it murmurings of peace and human security, yet it introduces an uncritical message of coming conflict which has since been a key theme of the literature.

In 1986 Myers explicitly argued for the incorporation of environmental issues into security thinking. Myers has argued consistently that environmental degradation will induce violent conflict:

> If a nation's environmental foundations are depleted, its economy will steadily decline, its social fabric deteriorate, and its political structure become destabilized. The outcome is all too likely to be conflict, whether conflict in the form of disorder and insurrection within the nation, or tensions and hostilities with other nations. (Myers 1986: 251)

Myers considers food shortages, fisheries depletion, water scarcity, climate change and deforestation to be issues likely to induce conflict. Environmental refugees also figure prominently. Despite the assertion that 'the linkages [to conflict] are readily apparent', the causal chain by which these issues might lead to conflict is not explicated (Myers 1986: 252). Indeed, Myers seems aware of this causality paradox: 'While certain of the linkages are diffuse in their workings, hence difficult to discern in their immediate operation, they are nonetheless real and important, and growing increasingly significant in their number and extent' (Myers 1986: 253). On the 'nature of linkages' Myers offers this explanation:

> [E]nvironmental deficiencies supply conditions that render conflict all the more likely. They can serve to determine the source of conflict, they can act as multipliers that can aggravate core causes of conflict. Moreover they can not only contribute to conflict, they can stimulate the growing use of force to repress disaffection of those who suffer the consequences of environmental decline. (Myers 1986: 253)

This is no explanation at all. Instead what is offered is a reassertion of the assumption that environmental change will lead to conflict. This is a trend that is repeated throughout most of the literature which seeks to explain the links between environmental change and conflict. The danger is that if the assumption is made often enough, it becomes reality.

What Myers *does* do well is explore the financial trade-offs between environmental problems and national security, arguing that money spent on the environment provides more security than money spent on the military. However, such arguments are unlikely to be effective, given that they follow lengthy discussions of the threats to the nation from the outside (such as refugees or wars) which may well involve military engagement. There is thus a political naivety here that endangers the environmental cause. The particular combination of issues (conflict with demilitarisation) is analytically incongruent as it does more to mobilise the institutions of national security than it does to threaten them with a green peace dividend.

In contrast to the emphasis on conflict in Myers's paper, in the same year (1986) Westing entered into the debate with a more peace-promoting discussion of the connections between environment and security (Westing 1986). Westing's focus is on preventing resource wars, and on using environmental measures to strengthen international security. Westing was an early proponent of cooperation (common security) on environmental issues among states:

> It is thus inescapable that any concept of international security must in the last analysis be based on this obligate relationship of humankind with its

environment .... Accordingly, it is necessary that consistent with the concept of equitable utilisation of shared natural resources, States co-operate with a view to controlling, preventing, reducing or eliminating adverse environmental effects which may result from the utilization of such resources. (Westing 1986: 195)

There is a sense in Westing's early analysis that development should be conducted in as environmentally benign a way as possible. This was precisely the theme of the World Commission on Environment and Development's *Our Common Future* (WCED 1987). Because it identifies with the earlier Brandt and Palme reports, it is not surprising that *Our Common Future* made much of the links between environmental degradation and security (see ICDSI 1982; ICIDI 1980, 1983). The WCED revisited key themes of the earlier literature, including the connection between environmental stress and conflict, and the need for cooperative international arrangements. It also made much of the environmental impacts of war, particularly those arising from the potential use of nuclear weapons. Significantly, the WCED report is seemingly the first explicitly to use the term environmental security.

The environmental security literature expanded significantly after 1989, when (at least) ten articles on the subject were published. This increased juxtaposition of security and environment came at a time when conventional understandings of security were no longer so obviously politically relevant (owing in large part to the decline of the Cold War), and when environmental issues were increasingly in the forefront of public concern (Dalby 1992). Indeed, according to Smil, environmental security has replaced the threat of global nuclear warfare as it shares two characteristics: both are global in reach and the effects of both could be highly devastating (Smil 1997).

Of these ten papers, Mathews's 'Redefining Security' (1989) warrants brief discussion. Mathews's paper emphasised the transboundary character of environmental problems and the challenge this presents to sovereign states. It also placed on the environmental security agenda the complex issue of biodiversity which has, by and large, remained unaddressed (suggesting that the prevailing approach is unable to cope with issues that defy its inside/outside and threat rationality). The paper was notable for its presence in *Foreign Affairs*, an established US foreign policy journal. Publishing there meant Mathews was taking aim at 'White House policymakers, the Cabinet agencies, the Pentagon, the US

Congress, and relevant interests groups and thinktanks' – in short, the US security policy community (Lipschutz 1995: 5). Mathews was seeking, then, to elevate environmental concerns to the level of security issues – in effect to 'securitise' environmental problems such that they might be accorded higher priority on the policy agenda.

A particularly notable and influential exposition of the environment as a security issue is Kaplan's 'The Coming Anarchy', published in *The Atlantic Monthly* in 1994. Kaplan's paper is said to have been widely read in the White House, and is reported to have made an impact on President Clinton (Dalby 1996a). Kaplan's is a doomsday prophecy and an ethno-centric and fundamentally realist account of the world. He seeks to depict 'what the political character of our planet is likely to be in the twenty-first century' (1994: 45). His 'premonition of the future' includes 'disease, overpopulation, unprovoked crime, scarcity of resources, refugee migra-tions, the increasing erosion of nation-states and international borders, and the empowerment of private armies, security firms, and international drug cartels' (Kaplan 1994: 44 and 46). 'The Coming Anarchy' speaks of 'the environment as a hostile power', saying that 'nature is coming back with a vengeance, tied to population growth', and making the bold assertion that 'it is time to understand the environment for what it is: *the national security issue of the twenty-first century*' (Kaplan 1994: 54, 60 and 58). Thus the environment is the villain in Kaplan's account of the world to come (Dalby 1996a: 472). Smil says Kaplan 'preaches with con-viction and with the simplistic zeal of a prophet', and that 'his conclusions are based on unqualified generalisations unmindful of enormous environ-mental and socio-economic peculiarities (Smil 1997: 124). 'The Coming Anarchy' is comprehensively critiqued by Dalby (1996a):

> Kaplan is in some ways a continuation of long-established lines of argument. But he is new in that his powerful articulation of environment as the cause of threats to national security has updated Malthusian themes and brought the 'environmental security' policy discussions forcefully to the attention of a wider public. In doing so Kaplan revisits many of the geopolitical assumptions in security thinking, and does so in specifying the environment as a cause of threat.... In the case of neo-Malthusianism and the more general policy dis-course of 'environmental security', the 'threat' is often at least partly from somehow external 'natural' or 'environmental' phenomena. (Dalby 1996a: 475)

'The Coming Anarchy' is not so much an extreme exception as it is the logical conclusion of the crude interpretation of environmental degradation as a national security threat. Its reputed success with the US President is indicative of the US approach to security policy, a point worth keeping in mind in the appraisal of US environmental security policy in Chapter 6.

The Environment and National Security

The bulk of environment and security reasoning starts from pre-existing and well-established theoretical and policy frameworks for national security, and then factors in environmental issues. Putting the emphasis on environmental issues and then relating these to security, however, suggests that there are some alternative grounds upon which the environment might be considered as a national security issue. First, the economic base that determines military capacity is itself underwritten by the natural environment. If the natural capital base of an economy erodes, then so does the long-term ability to defend against external aggression (it follows, then, that economic and military strength may not be complete measures of national security). In this sense, the ability of the North to transfer environmental externalities to the South helps the Northern economies to maintain their natural capital base, therefore sustaining economic growth and military superiority. Thus if economic development can be ecologically unsustainable, then national security can be similarly unsustainable.

There is a second, more general connection between national security and environmental degradation which stems from the frequent reference to the 'national interest' in security policy. Environmental degradation has many and complex negative effects on the national interest. It threatens individual and collective economic livelihoods by eroding the natural capital base of the economy; it affects health through contamination of water, air and food; it exposes humans to new health risks by disrupting ecological processes; it reduces the overall quality of life; and it exacerbates inequalities between people.

In Australia, for example, environmental degradation is arguably the biggest threat to the national interest. Since European settlement Australia has lost 75 per cent of its tropical forests (Bolt 1992: 90); 306 species of native plants and 47 species of native animals are presumed extinct or threatened with extinction (Boyden and Shirlow 1990: 142); in many parts of the country drinking water quality doesn't meet World Health Organisation guidelines (Nix 1990); and in urban areas in particular air pollution is undermining health (Commonwealth of Australia 1992:

109). Further, given that three quarters of Australia's population lives on the coastal fringe, the very real prospect of sea-level rise caused by global warming is a serious threat to Australia's interests and way of life. Even a single organism could wreak havoc: for example, foot and mouth disease could cause rural output to decline by $6 billion in the first year alone (Commonwealth of Australia 1993: 19). Bolt (1992) compares land degradation with military invasion in terms of relative likelihood and impact, and finds that land degradation imposes a greater overall cost on the Australian economy than military invasion due to its continued recurrence; in 1990 the cost of land degradation in Australia was $1.2 billion in lost agricultural production alone (Bolt 1992: 102). In terms of loss of territory, over half of Australia's land surface suffers from some form of land degradation, an impact unlikely to be matched by any foreseeable type of military engagement. Thus 'it can reasonably be concluded that the security of Australia and Australians is far more at risk from environmental pressures than from military threat' (Bolt 1992: 104). This analysis questions the efficacy of Australia's present security and defence policies and the selective view of threats and impacts upon which these are premised.

A third connection between environmental degradation and national security comes from the recognition that national boundaries have little meaning with respect to environmental problems. This is of relevance to national security as transboundary environmental problems 'challenge the primacy of the sovereign state actor in safeguarding territory, populations and interests' (Dabelko and Dabelko 1995: 9). Transboundary flows differ from traditional external security threats in that they are uncontrolled and most often unintended, in this respect they are 'threats without enemies' (Prins 1993). Climate change, for example, undermines national security in important ways. For the four Pacific atoll-states of Kiribati, the Marshall Islands, Tokelau and Tuvalu, climate change is a security issue of a magnitude unprecedented in the history of nation-states, as rising sea levels and heightened climatic variability threaten their functional viability.

The understanding that environmental problems are national security issues is not unproblematic. According to Jervis, who plays upon the uncertainties inherent in natural science predictions, environmental problems are 'too far off, the scientific evidence is too ambiguous, the domestic interests involved are too conflicting, and the alternative approaches are too many' (1991: 64). It is Deudney, however, who questions the linking of environmental degradation and national security most compellingly (Deudney 1990, 1992). He offers three reasons why the linkage is analytically misleading. First, he argues that military threats are patently different from environmental threats, particularly in that military threats are deliberately imposed; as Prins eloquently puts it: 'you can't shoot an ozone hole' (Prins 1991: 2). Deudney suggests that national security logic is incapable of grasping environmental issues or dealing with them effectively. This is for the most part true in so far as national security continues to be the domain of the military – and it seems particularly true in the US context in which Deudney writes. Few authors outside of the military/security establishment, however, suggest that a traditional security response is required to meet environmental problems. The overwhelming message from non-military commentaries is that a redefinition of security is required, and that common security should be the preferred paradigm. In this respect Deudney perhaps misses the point of the literature, but in as much as realist conceptions of security prevail, Deudney's point is not invalidated.

Deudney's second argument against linking environmental degradation and national security is that declaring 'environmental changes as a threat to national security (as many environmental activists do) in order to mobilise action may be counterproductive and produce undesirable side-effects' (1992: 171). This is undoubtedly Deudney's most important contribution to the literature, and it is a concern which cannot be easily dismissed. Brock (1991, 1997) and Lipschutz (1992b) have also noted this dilemma (see chapters 6 and 7). Finally, Deudney's third argument against environmental security as it applies to the nation-state is that 'environmental degradation is not very likely to cause interstate wars' (1990: 461). This is discussed in the following chapter.

There is therefore some basis for considering environmental problems as national security problems, not least because the state is the principal and most powerful institution in existence. Nevertheless, the interpretation of what constitutes national security, who it is for, and how it is to be achieved is still the central problematic. Many of the more environmentally oriented bases for considering the environment as a national security issue are ignored or downplayed because national security is still interpreted in a narrow and abstract way to mean the security of the nation (not so much its constituents) from external contingencies, to be attained by the application of military, diplomatic and economic power.

Common and comprehensive security

A theme of the literature on redefining security is that environmental degradation requires collective action. That a common security approach is required is self-evident given the transboundary character of some forms of environmental degradation. This leaves little choice for policy but to act in a framework of common security, and to act in such a way as to prevent the onset of environmental problems which have a trans-boundary character. On issues with a regional or bilateral impact and a relatively identifiable cause, such as acid rain, a common security approach is likely to be successful (Carroll 1989). With a global issue such as climate change, however, where there is uncertainty and complexity, and where tracing causes and effects exposes differences in responsibility and impact, effective action and common security may be less easy to achieve (as the Australian government's refusal to adhere to standard carbon accounting procedures as laid down in the UN Framework Convention on Climate Change indicates). Common environmental problems are far more intractable than those issues that have traditionally been the domain of common security; hence, whilst environmental problems fit easily into the common security framework, the framework itself may be in need of fundamental reform to be truly effective on environmental issues.

While a common security approach makes sense, more profound changes to resolve environmental insecurity are also required. A number of authors have advocated a comprehensive security approach which involves linking environmental security initiatives with a broader array of complementary activities. For example Kakonen argues that 'under-development and the phenomena connected with it, as well as environ-mental problems, are phenomena of destruction caused by development. In other words, different threats are closely connected to a set of values and a way of life' (Kakonen 1992: 147–8). Thus comprehensive security must entail more than a superficial linkage of issues within a framework of common security; it must involve widespread and deep reform of modern society. This line of thinking is no doubt correct; environmental problems cannot be seen in isolation from development and economic issues, and any serious attempt to provide environmental security requires addressing the broad array of causes of environmental degradation.

Linking environmental issues into a common and comprehensive security framework has implications for existing international institutions.

Various options have been proposed, including new international institutions such as a United Nations (UN) environmental security council, and a green cross or green UN police force (Schrijver 1989). The most immediate option, however, is to reform and strengthen existing institutions, and it is here that Imber's work on UN reform has much to offer (Imber 1994). Despite an array of criticisms about the UN, Imber is positive about its potential role, arguing that 'the UN *is* the appropriate forum for much necessary environmental diplomacy', and that it is 'the only place in which all the world's states can meet ... to negotiate new norms of behaviour and adopt binding conventions on a range of issues' (Imber 1994: 211, 114). He suggests that the UN is well suited to certain tasks, including the collection and dissemination of large data sets, the consensus negotiation of norms, establishing rules of law, and monitoring compliance with environmental regulations. This optimistic view of the role of the UN is generally justified. Certainly, despite many shortcomings, the UN has been crucial to the promotion of environmental concerns on the global agenda and, given the difficulties of international diplomacy, it must surely have a key role to play in ongoing efforts to provide environmental security.

A salient point about common security is that for the most part responsibility still rests with nations who are urged to act to secure their common interests. It thus works by extending the logic of national security, and does not challenge the legitimacy of the nation-state's domination of political life.

Redefining security: what's at stake?

The most important critique of expanded conceptions of security, of which environmental considerations are part, concerns the possibility of militarised responses. Because the prevailing approach to security is still 'mired in ideological straitjackets', and carries with it an array of sentiments and a narrow problem-solving mindset, its utility for comprehending and responding to non-military issues is questionable (Dalby 1991: 29). When examining discourses of 'the war on drugs', 'water wars', Third World turbulence and so on, it becomes increasingly apparent that this post-Cold War security agenda is still basically the same realist agenda that prevailed throughout the Cold War, although now exhibiting previously secondary concerns brought forth in the sudden absence of the mobilising West–East threat. Campbell argues that the Western response to the current era of world politics is 'characterised by the representation of novel challenges in terms of traditional analytics, and the varied attempts to replace one enemy with (an)other' (Campbell 1992: 8). This is borne out in the 1998 US National Security Strategy which states that 'the current international security environment presents a diverse set of threats to our enduring goals and hence to our security', including transnational threats such as 'terrorism, international crime, drug trafficking, illicit arms trafficking, uncontrolled refugee migrations and environmental damage' which 'threaten US interests, citizens and the US homeland itself' (Clinton 1998: 10). A key part of the US response is to 'maintain superior military forces at the level of readiness necessary to effectively deter aggression, conduct a wide range of peacetime activities and smaller-scale contingencies, and, preferably in concert with regional friends and allies, win two overlapping major theater wars' (Clinton 1998: 11).

This holds true for environmental security as well, as Smil argues:

> In thinking about the new horse of environmental degradation, it is really the old gibbon's heart of national security that many of the new securitarians want to preserve. They alter, dilute, and extend the meaning of security beyond any classical recognition, but they never give up on its original idea which embodies conflict and violence. This is because the idea carries them to the heart of existential anguish and moral peril, fears without which their message would not merit such an anxious hearing by politicians, the military, or the mass media. (Smil 1997: 108)

Thus the hidden goal of security – that of maintaining power within the state – remains unchallenged so long as security is projected as an absolute imperative. In short, the effect of broadening national security to include social, political and environmental issues – without changing the nation-state as the referent – is the further colonisation of domestic society by realism's ultimately violent logic.

For as long as security remains tied up in the state-centric realist paradigm, introducing new issues will be conceptually counterintuitive and practically counterproductive to these issues, and to the broader goal of justice. In most of the accounts discussed in this chapter, the logical confines of conventional security reasoning are not broken, and the state remains *the* site of politics. So, adding new issues to the agenda of security studies does not necessarily equate to a modification of the conceptual base, and may lead to a bolstering of the state-centred approach (Shaw 1993). Expanding the security agenda without seriously contesting the meaning of security perpetuates the failure of the security concept to take into account the needs of people. In this broader (but not deeper) agenda, security is still the preserve of states acting in their own interests – interests which for the most part do not correspond to the needs of people.

Yet the expansion of the concept of security is only malignant for as long as security equates with national security attained through military strategy. There are a range of other definitions of security that identify alternative referents (discussed in chapters 8 and 9). These do more than expand the meaning of security; they seek to reclaim it by deepening the concept until it speaks to the security needs of people (not nations), and by addressing risk and uncertainty in accommodating and adaptive ways. Even given these radical approaches, it remains an open and ongoing question as to whether the notion of security is too thoroughly contaminated with associations of power and violence to warrant further use. This issue is taken up again in Chapter 9, where the advantages and disadvantages of securitising environmental problems are considered.

Despite some good intentions, the search for new security issues has led to the discursive reinvigoration of the state and its self-appointed protectors via the continued construction of Others and discourses of danger. In this context it is not surprising that we read that 'environmental degradation is becoming (along with extreme nationalism, religious radicalism, and economic conflict) a prime threat for the 21st century' (Winnefeld and Morris 1994: 2). The origination of this discourse of environment as a threat can be attributed largely to Ullman and Myers, who presented environmental insecurity in terms of conflict and danger to the nation. This issue of conflict and the environment is discussed in the following chapter.

5

Environmental Degradation
and Conflict
Conscripting the Voice of Dissent

The contention that environmental degradation will lead to violent conflict is central to most interpretations of environmental security. A number of broad trends are identified as increasing the likelihood of environmentally induced conflicts, including: expanding and migrating human populations; water, arable land and other resource and environmental scarcities; ongoing militarisation; globalisation which brings people (and diseases) into closer proximity; and increasing recognition of the injustice of Northern-induced underdevelopment of the South. Most of these trends are neither novel nor environmental. The critical issue for the study of environmental security is whether, and how, environmental degradation triggers violent conflict. There is little if any evidence to suggest that environmental problems do cause violent conflict; instead what is presented are theories that have intuitive appeal but empirically fail to convince. Despite this, the environment–conflict thesis influences national security discourse and subsequent policy in important ways, particularly in the United States. That security strategists propose such theories is not surprising given the ongoing search for new threats to justify old institutions; there is, however, a weighty contribution from biophysical scientists as well. In this sense, potential dissenters to the militarisation of environmental problems have been conscripted (if indeed they have not opted) into the service of established institutions.

Resource wars

The causes and consequences of 'resource wars' are traditional concerns of international relations, and these powerfully inform the environment–conflict thesis. For example, for Gleick 'a strong argument can be made linking certain resource and environmental problems with prospects for war or peace. There is a long history suggesting that access to resources is a proximate cause of war' (Gleick 1990: 507). A pervasive difficulty with this literature is the conflation of *resources* with *environment*. First, with respect to the question of resource scarcity, it is worth noting that scarcity is a relative phenomenon; the problem in most cases comes from the expectation of abundance which is denied for structural reasons rather than natural ones (Bookchin 1982). Second, the literature is by and large concerned with resources of economic value rather than with environmental issues *per se*. For example, Francisco Magno argues that tensions in the South China Sea fit 'well within the framework of environmental security.... The expansion of economic activity, mixed with the depletion of natural resources in the region, has intensified the scramble for resources' (Magno 1997: 100). Magno reflects the traditional international relations concern with war over resources; the environmental dimensions are not particularly evident. Robert Mandel explicitly conflates resources with environment in his chapter 'Resource/Environmental Security'; in a revealing passage he says that 'analyzing the link between resource/environmental concerns and national security without a foundation in the substantial geopolitical literature would be foolhardy' (Mandel 1994: 77). Thus, for Mandel as for many others, resource and environmental issues are one and the same; they are of interest only in as much as they relate to national security, and the key to understanding them lies in the study of traditional geopolitical texts.

This confusion of resources with environment is perhaps most clear in Gleick's work. Gleick argues that there are five 'clear connections' between environmental degradation and security: '*resources* as strategic goals, *resources* as strategic targets; *resources* as strategic tools; *resource* inequities as roots to conflict; and environmental services and conditions as roots to conflict' (Gleick 1990: 508, my emphasis). Of these, only one speaks directly to environmental issues, the first four are themes of well-established resource–conflict research. Gleick's argument is characteristic of the strategic rationality that is increasingly resurfacing under the rubric of 'environment' in the new security era. A notable function of this conflation of resource scarcities with environmental issues is that it offers strategic rationality a beachhead on the environmental agenda because resources and conflict are central to the strategic stock-in-trade.

It is important, then, to make the distinction between resource scarcity and environmental disturbance clearer to provide a membrane (albeit at times porous) against the inappropriate colonisation of environmental issues by the resource/strategy agenda. To begin, it is worth restating Julian Simon's basic argument that economic processes can account for scarcity through price mechanisms and substitution (Simon 1981). To be sure, Simon's argument is not valid in all circumstances; one important caveat is that there are circumstances where technology and the market are not induced to find substitutes, such as in the case of localised depletions of clean water or fuelwood in industrialising countries. The point of revisiting Simon's theory is to say that resource scarcity is not the most pressing *environmental* problem, and to suggest that there are some substantive differences between resource and environmental problems.

The most complex, uncertain, and potentially disruptive problems lie not in the realm of environmental sources but in silent, apolitical and pervasive processes which are overloading the planetary 'sinks' (see McMichael 1993: 47). Accordingly, a rule of thumb in most of the cited instances of resource scarcity is that, where the scarce resource can be costed and its price altered according to the balance of supply and demand, and if necessary substituted, the problem is more *economic* than it is *environmental*. Environmental problems are those effects or externalities that cannot be costed or reasonably substituted, such as increasing rates of pollution-induced cancer, biodiversity losses, and the effects of climate change. These issues are already discernible in declining human security, felt mostly by the already insecure. These are the essence of environmental insecurity. Water and soils are two basic resources that defy this classification, having both economic and ecological functions; as argued below, however, arguments that there will be 'water wars' are also unconvincing, and the issue of land degradation has yet to be seriously considered as a cause of conflict.

The prospect of war over resources is dubious even without considering environmental factors. Lipschutz and Holdren advance the liberal argument that military action to secure access to resources is unlikely given the interdependence among states in the global economy (Lipschutz and Holdren 1990). They suggest that war is less cost-effective than pursuing the same goal through trade, that technological advances have increased the substitutability of materials, and that raw materials are now less important to economic success. At the same time as dismissing the possibility of war over economic resources, however, Lipschutz and Holdren argue that environmental problems now pose 'the greatest threats to international stability' (1990: 126). Yet one can argue that if thus far the oppressed and exploited in the South have not resorted to force as a means to free themselves from the underdevelopment imposed by the North, it seems questionable to assume that they will do so in the future on the basis of additional environmental pressures. In short, if the argument that interdependence promotes peace holds for resource-based conflicts, then arguably it holds equally for environmentally based conflicts. Thus even in more critical works such as Lipschutz and Holdren's the ontological priority is still given to conflict before cooperation, and there are still nuances of the determinism that attaches itself to environmental problems.

The environment–conflict literature is almost entirely premised on the ethnocentric assumption that people in the South will resort to violence in times of resource scarcity. Rarely, if ever, is the same argument applied to people in the industrialised North. There is continued scripting of people from the South as barbaric, strongly implying that those in the North are more civilised. Nevertheless, the former Yugoslavia excepted, there may indeed be a degree of institutional/social resilience in industrialised societies that hedges against large-scale violence most of the time, and this, at least, offers hope as a meaningful research agenda for environmental security. There are at least three possible reasons for the resilience of industrialised societies. First, as the industrialised economies partake of the global division of labour and resources they effect a global division of environmental degradation as well, thereby transferring environmental degradation abroad. Given this, environmental security seems to involve securing the ecological health of the nation by transferring environmental externalities. Second, the levels of wealth in the industrialised world – wealth gained through the exploitation of cheap labour and materials abroad – allows for institutions that provide stability and resilience to environmental change. The market, well-financed government, the insurance industry, transport and communications infrastructure, a degree of democratic participation, and a base level of personal affluence all seem to help hedge against turmoil in the face of environmental stress. Third, trade between similarly affluent liberal democracies assists in the transfer of necessary food and technology that helps enhance resilience and decreases the likelihood of rivalry. Underwriting all this, however, is the ability to pay and to participate in the domestic and global economy without great disadvantage. This ability, of course, is limited to the few and underwritten by the exploitation of the many.

This brings us to a pervasive analytical difficulty of the literature which posits the possibility of environmentally induced conflicts. If, as Gleick suggests, 'developing countries have far fewer technical and economic resources at their disposal', and hence are less able to adapt to environmental change, then this institutional impoverishment surely applies to their ability to wage war as well (Gleick 1990: 518). The threat from the South could scarcely manifest itself as large-scale warfare, despite Gleick's observation that 'Third World arms capabilities are impressive and growing' and so 'the threat to peace and security becomes fully apparent' (1990: 519). There may indeed be some possibility of low-intensity conflict driven by desperation over and resentment of the policies and practices of the North, but it is important to step back and view the broader picture. The revealing question is *whose peace and security?* The absolute peace and security problem is not that in the face of intolerable oppression the oppressed may resist; the problem is the oppression and injustice itself. The task, then, is to eliminate this injustice rather than prepare to defend against its possible ramifications.

The real irony of the environment–conflict literature is that it is the industrialised world which assumes that the South will threaten. The North creates its own fiction, based on little or no evidence; Northern strategic vision projects onto the industrialising world its own violent rationality. It assumes that the South will behave as the North tends to, that is with aggression and force. Yet this is merely an assumption; there may be rogue states (Iraq, Libya, North Korea), but these few are exceptions and do not represent the vast majority of industrialising states. Hence the 'threat to peace and security' which is 'fully apparent' to Gleick is by no means obvious. The peace and security being referred to is the peace and security of the industrialised states, not the positive peace and security to which the majority of the world's people are entitled. This Northern peace is a negative peace, and its security is a resistance to change.

Water wars

A consistent concern of the environmental security literature is the likelihood of conflict over water (see for example Cooley 1984, Gleick 1993,

Myers 1996, Starr 1991). According to Joyce Starr, for example, 'water security will soon rank with military security in the war rooms of defense ministries'; and for Barry Buzan 'it is not difficult to imagine the issue of allocations of water along rivers such as the Nile, the Mekong and the Indus becoming causes for the use of military force' (Starr 1991: 19; Buzan 1991: 132). The literature makes much of the observation that 261 major river systems are shared by two or more countries (Wolf et al., 1999). Naff (1992: 25) exemplifies the reasoning that underlies the water wars thesis: 'In sum, the strategic reality of water is that under circumstances of scarcity, it becomes a highly symbolic, contagious, aggregated, intense, salient, complicated, zero-sum, power- and prestige-packed issue, highly prone to conflict and extremely difficult to resolve.'

There is a typical pattern to the water wars argument: the geographical misfit between water and national boundaries is explored; next, a healthy dose of 'practical geopolitical reasoning' is applied; then, despite having made much of the prospect of water wars, there is usually a brief discussion of remedial measures, which tends to read like an afterthought on the substantive issue of warfare (on practical geopolitical reasoning see O'Tuathail and Agnew 1992). The usual case in point is the Middle East, a region already rife with religious, ethnic and political tensions. For many authors water scarcity will be the proverbial spark that starts the metaphorical Middle East bonfire, which in turn is seen to threaten international security (see, for example, Bulloch and Darwish 1993, Gleick 1993, Winnefeld and Morris 1994).

A critical problem with the water wars thesis (and indeed all the environment–conflict literature) is the impossibility of clearly distinguishing among the many factors which contribute to warfare. When one sifts through the hyperbole, it seems that few wars have been induced by water shortages alone. As Lipschutz has observed, examples offered as evidence of wars over water tend to be about something else (Lipschutz 1992b). It seems that the broader political context is more relevant than the specific instance of water scarcity (Lowi 1996). Nevertheless, there appears to be sufficient evidence, particularly that provided by Homer-Dixon's research, that water is an important variable in violent conflict within, if not always between states (for a summary, see Homer-Dixon and Percival 1996). Further, in the case of conflict in the Middle East, pronouncements by the region's politicians identifying water as a cause of violence suggest that the prospect of water wars should be taken seriously.

Nevertheless, the argument about water wars is overstated, is a particular product of strategic rationality, and undervalues the historical and contemporary evidence that water is as likely to 'cement peace' as it is to induce violence (Cooley 1984: 3).

Authors concerned about water wars have made much of an observation by Boutros Boutros-Ghali (then Egyptian Foreign Minister) that 'the next war in our region will be over the waters of the Nile, not politics' (cited in Gleick 1991: 20). Yet if Clausewitz's dictum that 'war is the continuation of politics by other means' is still relevant, war over the waters of the Nile is still a war about politics. To put it another way, if there is conflict over water, then that conflict is the result of a failure of politics to negotiate a settlement over the shared use of water. The idea that a war over water, or any other resource, is not a war about politics is dubious. Politicians and military leaders might wish to present war in Darwinian or Malthusian terms as a fight over subsistence needs, but this 'state of nature' rhetoric is a pragmatic device that denies responsibility for peaceful action, and justifies violence in lieu of meaningful dialogue. The problem is enhanced when environmental scientists such as Gleick deploy a similarly unsophisticated and behaviourist attitude toward serious issues of war and peace, ignoring the responsibility of theorists to consider the implications of their work.

That much of the water wars literature is written by Northern commentators focusing on the Middle East is instructive. It suggests that the issue is important not because of an *a priori* concern for those people who may suffer from warfare (if it was we might see more discussion of the everyday problems of water scarcity as well), but because of the problems war in the Middle East might create for Northern interests in the region. The Middle East is certainly vulnerable to water shortages, but Central and Southern Africa have similar, if not worse, water scarcities and hydrological perturbations (as do Australia and Spain, among many countries so afflicted), as well as long-standing political and social tensions. Yet there is no superpower presence in Africa, no religion-infused threats to world order, and, perhaps most importantly, no media interest. Detailed geographic analyses of the issue of water scarcity in the Middle East by Beaumont (1997) and Lonergan (1997) find that there is indeed no reason to expect conflict over water in the near future. In sum, the sensationalist discourse on water wars in the Middle East seems motivated by Northern interests rather than a concern for the people or the environment in the region. More particularly, any discourse from the Northern security community which posits instability in the Middle East can be read as a primer to justify a Northern military presence which occurs under the name of 'peace' but is in the interests of oil.

Examination of water issues in Southern Africa might soon confound the water wars thesis. The Okavango River, for example, is a little-studied but useful case of the way in which water scarcity can lead to cooperation rather than war. The Okavango River is shared by Angola, Botswana and Namibia, and has important health, economic and ecological functions. As a result of impending tensions over scarce water resources, a commission was established by these three states in 1994. Since then, the commission has co-managed the river effectively and peacefully, demonstrating that water can form a common basis for peace (in so far as there has not been conflict between states).

The selection of cases to prove the water wars thesis is suspect. What is truly notable is the failure to examine successful and peaceful water management regimes, such as those in Western Europe and North America (with the exception of Correia and da Silva 1997, and Llamas 1997). This omission might be explained by an absence of scarcity, or the relative balance of military powers (although this is not the case with US–Mexico cooperation over the waters of the Colorado River), but the failure to examine positive cases might also be a function of the way in which warfare appeals to our sensationalist and militaristic culture. The water wars thesis can be read as a case of 'civilised' Europeans constructing a barbaric Other. It suggests that there is a pervasive lack of interest in peace, and that warfare is more interesting. Further, the focus on conflict rather than peace creates the justification for strategic interventions in key regions. In this respect 'environment' is part of the discursive repackaging of the Northern security agenda.

A counterargument to the prospect of water wars has come from Deudney, who argues that cooperation and co-management of water resources may be the more likely outcome of water scarcity (Deudney 1991). Empirical evidence for this is offered by Libiszewski (1997) who has argued that water has served as a focus for dialogue and confidence-building in the Middle East, an important if unpopular counterweight to the prophecies on water wars. This suggestion is supported by strategic considerations as well, namely that exploitation of water resources requires expensive and vulnerable engineering systems, creating a mutual hostage situation and thereby reducing the incentives for states to employ violence to resolve conflict (Deudney 1991: 26). In short, water is not likely to be a source of conflict because it is difficult to enclose securely.

Up until the advent of industrialisation, water was for the most part peacefully co-managed, refuting the deterministic assumption of violent defence of resources which underlies the water wars thesis. Indeed, water rights have always been a key mechanism for coping with water scarcity (Bennett and Dahlberg 1990). This is also true in the case of the Middle East, where there has been a complex system of water rights, and where water has been an integral part of traditional customs. Prior to the modern state, water was a basis for negotiation and cooperation, which suggests that, despite the impediments imposed by the state system, the peaceful management of water scarcity is still (culturally) possible.

Population, environment and conflict

Considerable attention has been paid to the links between population, the environment and conflict. The standard argument is that population growth will overextend the natural resources of the immediate environs, leading to deprivation which, it is assumed, will lead to conflict and insta- bility, either directly through competition for scarce resources, or indirectly through the generation of environmental refugees. For example, according to Myers: 'so great are the stresses generated by too many people making too many demands on their natural-resource stocks and their institutional support systems, that the pressures often create first-rate breeding grounds for conflict' (Myers, 1987: 16).

Although the ways in which population growth leads to environ- mental degradation are reasonably well known, with poverty being the central problem, the particular ways in which this leads to conflict are difficult to prove. In the absence of proof a negative style of argumenta- tion occurs, and there are blanket assertions and abrogations: 'the rela- tionship is rarely causative in a direct fashion', but 'we may surmise that conflict would not arise so readily, nor would it prove so acute, if the associated factor of population growth were occurring at a more manage- able rate' (Myers 1987: 16). Yet rather than inducing warfare, overpopu- lation tends to lead to famine, which in turn reduces the capacity of a people to wage war. To understand famine as a cause of warfare is to marginalise the more pressing process whereby warfare causes famine, and it denies the higher moral issue of the responsibility of the industrial-ised world to those in affected regions.

To focus on the conflict potential inherent in population growth is to ignore the real causes of poverty and vulnerability, namely the economic disadvantages people in the industrialising world experience from their exposure to global capital. Vulnerability to famine can be lessened through substantial increases in access to employment, health care, education for women and children, and contraception. Resilience to famine can be enhanced by protecting traditional societies from the dis-ruptive effects of modern society, by creating safe political conditions, and by permitting more autonomous governance at the local level. The consequences of famine can be lessened by making use of the efficient collection and delivery mechanisms that characterise world trade between industrialised nations to deliver necessary supplies. All these mainstream development concerns are ignored or treated as afterthoughts when the issue of population growth is understood as a probable cause of war.

This population–environment–conflict reasoning is captured in an early pronouncement by Robert MacNamara (former US Secretary of Defense and former President of the World Bank), who said in 1984 that: 'short of thermonuclear war itself, population growth is the gravest issue the world faces over the decades immediately ahead' (cited in Myers 1987: 15). We should be immediately suspicious when pronouncements likening population growth to nuclear war come from key figures in the Northern world order such as MacNamara. Whose 'world' is he referring to? If MacNamara the philanthropist is talking here about the plight of those who are adversely affected by rapid population growth and famine, then the 'world' in question may be that of the Southern people at the receiving end of the exploitative, poverty-making global economy. This world is at risk from those very institutions with which MacNamara is so familiar – the World Bank, the Pentagon, and Ford motor company. More probably, MacNamara the defence secretary is referring to the world of US interests and the possibility that the growth in the number of Others might undermine the stability of (Northern) world order. The world that MacNamara sees is particular to the vantage of power. His is the view that comes from directing aircraft carriers and satellites; from granting billion-dollar loans and shaping national economies to fit the global economy. The world he sees most clearly is the world of the wealthy and powerful, and this is the same world he seeks to protect.

There are three principal omissions associated with the population–environment–conflict literature. First, by scripting population growth in industrialising countries as a threat to the interests of the industrialised countries, it presents population growth as an issue which requires management by the industrial powers. It is not countenanced that this might involve the relinquishment or adjustment of economic power. Second, it assumes that the number of people is absolutely indicative of ecological impact. This totally ignores the question of what kinds of lifestyle these people lead. Overall environmental impact is not merely a function of numbers, but also a function of the resources people use and the wastes they generate: lifestyle is thus as important as the number of lives. From this point of view the most overpopulated country in the world is the United States, which has 4.7 per cent of the world's population, consumes 25 per cent of all processed minerals, and produces 24 per cent of the world's greenhouse gases. In contrast, an 'overpopulated' country like India has 16 per cent of the world's population, but consumes only 3 per cent of all minerals and produces around 4 per cent of greenhouse gases (after UNDP 1996 and Miller 1994). Hence overemphasising population as a cause of environmental degradation turns a blind eye to the complicity of industrialised nations.

Finally, by viewing population as a threat, by indicating this threat through impersonal demographic statistics, and by seeing it from a global perspective and in Malthusian terms, this literature ignores the social and biological aspects of birth (on Malthus and environmental security see Dalby 1996a). For the population doomsayers another birth is a negative incremental addition to the problem. Further, the life that comes from birth is seen to be miserable and burdensome. Yet high population growth in the industrialising world is generated in part by the realisation on the part of parents that prospects for survival are increased by having children. To be sure, other factors such as the exclusion of women from public life, inadequate maternal and postnatal medical care, unavailability of birth control devices and religious and cultural factors all play a part. Yet it is surely of some significance that having children is both socially rewarding and a matter of basic biological behaviour. Having children is one thing that people have always done. Giving birth and raising children demand non-instrumental modes of reason which involve a respect for life and community, nurturing, love, responsibility and a long-term focus on the future.

These positive aspects of population growth are wholly ignored by the population–environment–conflict literature.

The project on environment, population and security

Of all the literature that addresses the links between environmental degradation, population and conflict, the work by the Project on Environment, Population and Security at the University of Toronto is the most engaging and thoughtful. The project began in 1994 and aimed to answer three questions, namely: what is known about the links among population growth, renewable resource scarcities, migration and conflict? What can be known about these links? What are the critical methodological issues affecting research on these links? These questions can be understood as seeking to substantiate what I have thus far called the *assumption* that environmental disturbances will induce conflicts.

The project was based on an early paper by Homer-Dixon (1991), the key premise of which was that industrialising countries are more vulnerable than rich ones to environmental change, and so are more prone to environmentally induced conflicts. Homer-Dixon identified four causally interrelated effects of environmental degradation: reduced agricultural production, economic decline, population displacement, and disruption of regular and legitimised social relations. All of these effects are identified as possibly contributing to (usually violent) conflict. The Project on Environment, Population and Security is premised on Homer-Dixon's essentially positivist logic. Diagrammatic models are used to explain the hypothetical processes whereby environmental degradation will induce conflict (see Homer-Dixon 1992, 1995).

The Toronto Project carried out numerous case studies to answer its three principal research questions (a listing of these can be found in the back of Homer-Dixon and Percival 1996). These case studies are, to varying degrees, well-researched background briefings on the difficulties experienced in particular regions, although they are more like development case studies than cases of relevance to security studies. What they demonstrate is that inequitable distributions of renewable resources are exacerbated in times of scarcity, and that at such times elites may try to capture resources to secure their interests (they avoid the conflation of resources and environment discussed earlier by talking about 'renewable environmental resources'). This in turn leads to population displacement, often forcing people into more environmentally fragile areas, where the cycle may begin anew. The initial problem of environmental scarcity thus creates a cycle of enclosure, capture and displacement, and in such a cycle the potential for violent episodes increases. In Homer-Dixon's view, environmental disruptions are not immediate causes of conflict, but can at times be contributing factors. Other key findings are that societies adapt either by using their environmental resources more efficiently or by reducing their dependence on the scarce environmental resources, and that 'in either case, the capacity to adapt depends on the level of social and technical ingenuity available in the society' (Homer-Dixon and Percival 1996: 7). It is also argued that failure to adapt results in impoverishment, migration, and weakening of the state, and that this may 'sharpen distinctions among groups and enhance their opportunities to participate in violent collective action' (Homer-Dixon and Percival 1996: 8). Finally, and contrary to the allegations of others, the project found that 'environmental scarcity rarely contributes directly to interstate conflict' (Homer-Dixon and Percival 1996: 9).

In terms of the broader literature it is important to note that this research has shifted attention away from global and regional issues to local issues. It offers a scale of analysis which was previously ignored by environment and security scholarship, but which is surely equally valid. It is also significant in that it dismisses the suggestion that environmental degradation will lead to conflict between states. To stress the key point, however, this research has not shown conclusively that violent conflict inevitably flows from environmental degradation, nor even that environmental degradation is a principle cause of violence. What it has shown is that environmental problems are contributing to social disturbances, which may involve violence or, less sensationally but no less importantly, more structural forms of disadvantage.

There are methodological difficulties when positivist social scientists such as Homer-Dixon engage in simplified, linear and positivist interpretations of the complex and uncertain interface between social and ecological systems. Vaclav Smil has called this rough-and-ready approach a form of 'environmental determinism', which does indeed seem an appropriate label (Smil 1997: 109). The popularity of this research no doubt stems from this pseudo-scientific approach. These problems of interdisciplinarity flow both ways, however: positivist and linear styles of analysis also characterise the work of Gleick and Myers, both of whom are biophysical scientists engaging in political commentary, and both of whom evince a crude environmental-determinist outlook. As suggested earlier, the errors of this latter pair are perhaps less excusable. Their role should be less about dramatising the prospect of environmentally induced conflicts, and more about providing credible and qualified scientific advice with reserved – if any – commentary on the political ramifications of environmental change.

One of the debates about environmental security concerns Marc Levy's criticism of Homer-Dixon's research. Levy is generally dismissive of all the environment and security literature, although his review of it is far from comprehensive (Levy 1995a and 1995b). He is particularly ungenerous in his regard for Homer-Dixon's work, arguing that it is 'bland' and offers nothing substantially new to security studies, although it should be noted that Homer-Dixon for the most part was not talking about security *per se*, focusing instead on conflict and violence. Levy is also overly concerned with the implications of Homer-Dixon's research for 'contemporary US security policy', another aspect that Homer-Dixon did not purport to address (Levy 1995a: 55).

Levy argues that the cases Homer-Dixon selected for study are all instances where there have been violent episodes, claiming that cases were selected to prove the initial assumption that environmental degradation may induce conflict. He suggests that an approach which compares different violent outcomes in similar circumstances would have been more appropriate. Yet it seems questionable to assume that two similar cases can be found, given different ecological, cultural, and political contexts. What is most interesting is Levy's implicit suggestion that a case is not worth studying unless there is some element of violent conflict. The issue for Levy, then, is the need to examine the factors that explain different levels of violent conflict, and not the need to examine those factors which might explain the *absence* of conflict altogether. An alternative and more revealing strategy would be to examine cases without a violent outcome. This would shift the emphasis away from reaction to adaptation, and would be more likely to lead to positive and long-term responses.

The crux of this debate on core methodological issues seems to hinge on the attempt by both Levy and Homer-Dixon to speak in positivist vernacular about an issue which cannot be explained by positivist research strategies. This aspect of the debate is most useful as a demonstration of the frustrations associated with an adherence to narrow social science dictums. Finally, at the risk of overstating the claim, it must again be noted that this excess of attention (from Homer-Dixon but even more so from Levy) to violent conflict steers the issue of environmental security in a direction which suits the national security establishment, and which does not offer much for further empirical research. From the normative and peace perspective outlined in Chapter 1 of this book, the issues that ought to be of more concern are the day-to-day insecurities associated with the erosion of individual and group welfare and resilience.

Despite a sensitivity to complexity, and despite the shift of focus away from the international to the local scale, the Toronto Project still said little about the fundamental question of what makes people resort to violence? This pivotal question, albeit difficult to answer, is one which the positivist methodology of Homer-Dixon is incapable of answering. The discussion of pressures, scarcities and conflict depicts the circum-stances and the conducive factors, but there is a leap of analysis from these to the decision to resort to force. In effect the key question – why fight? – cannot be wholly explained by compiling a litany of pressures. Were this wholly sufficient to explain the likelihood of violence, Gandhi would have preached bloody revolution and Mandela would have opted for militant retribution. Perhaps the more telling question to be examined, then, is why do people *not* resort to violence? Hence, to repeat, a more productive research agenda would be to examine cases where, in the face of similar pressures, violence was not the end product (rather than cases where there were lesser degrees of violence as Levy suggests).

Homer-Dixon's research 'provides additional support for a range of policies – from selective debt relief to enhancement of indigenous technical capacity – that many development experts have long recognised as valuable' (Homer-Dixon and Percival 1996: 4). This is important despite Levy's suggestion that it is 'banal advice' which does not identify 'key intervention points' (a profoundly dismissive attitude towards con-ventional wisdom about redressing environment and development problems) (Levy 1995a: 57). Although not the emphasis of Homer-Dixon's work, the point is that strategies for peace, justice, development and sustainability are necessary for there to be security. The implication is that there is little connection between environmental degradation and security when security is understood as a national concern. Instead, the problem of environmental insecurity is a problem of underdevelopment. This is the subversive message of Homer-Dixon's work. It adds impetus to the argument that environmental problems only have meaning for security if security is understood in *human* terms.

Theoretical deficiencies

The argument that environmental degradation will induce violent conflict over scarce resources recasts ecological problems in mainstream international relations terms; it scripts the South as primeval Other, and as a consequence suggests the imposition of the North to maintain order. The water wars thesis is no less ethnocentric in outlook, and it is here that we see most clearly the deployment of environment issues in the rewriting of security to justify longstanding interventions in regions of strategic importance, particularly the Middle East. That it is unconvincing in its assertion that there will be large-scale violent conflict over water further highlights this book's claim that the environment–conflict thesis is a poor theoretical justification for security business-as-usual. The selective interpretation continues in the argument that when population growth exceeds ecological limits, conflict will ensue. Here, the most immediate development and human security issues are peripheral to strategic concerns about civil conflicts and refugees. Again, the interpretation is of the South, by the North.

As a body of theory, the environment–conflict literature reflects the intermingling of neo-realist and liberal theories in North American security discourse, a confluence which excludes alternative critical perspectives and which, ironically in the case of environmental security, serves to marginalise the insights of a Green theory. At this point some further critical observations about environment–conflict theory are warranted.

History

There is a consistent lack of historical perspective in the environment–conflict literature. There is no clear appreciation of the long history leading up to contemporary environmental insecurities. This a fundamental failing given that it is the broader social and ecological degradation wrought by modernity which is the overriding context for any discussion of security and social tension. Thus Smil writes that 'any thoughtful historian, and especially those fascinated by the complex relationships between civilisations and their environment, must be astonished by the utter neglect of long term historical perspectives' (Smil 1997: 107). There is also a lack of historical contextualisation in the specific cases where environmental degradation is thought to have been a factor in violent conflict. Even a recent history of these places would more than likely reveal the vitally important factors of unequal terms of trade, structural adjustment programmes, colonial and post-colonial imperialism, and the influence of Northern values and aspirations on non-Northern cultures. Yet all these and other factors are rarely acknowledged.

The most important thing about the use of history in this environment–conflict literature is the way many authors pick and choose historical evidence in a way that highlights the negative instances whilst ignoring the positive. Various historical examples are offered as evidence for the tendency of humans to go to war over resources. The issue is less whether there were environmental dimensions to past conflicts, although this may be questioned given the difficulty of proving the case even in contemporary times. The more pertinent issue is whether history is not a biased record, one that tells us far more about violence than it does about peace (Gandhi 1951). As a body of evidence to support an argument about the preponderance of violent behaviour, history is suspect. A more balanced and productive use of history would include discussion of those cultures that have lived sustainably and in peace. The overarching message of history is that humans as individuals and as a species continually adapt and survive, and are therefore able to adapt to environmental pressures (Boyden 1987). This historical perspective stands as perhaps the greatest counterfactual to declarations of 'the coming anarchy' (Kaplan's term, 1994).

The nature of nature

Underlying the environment–conflict literature is a set of essentialised readings of human (internal) and external nature. It has already been suggested that there is a form of environmental determinism involved. This arises for the most part from the involvement of biophysical scientists (such as Gleick and Myers) commenting on matters of political science informed by a Malthusian 'laws of nature' cosmology; and of political scientists such as Homer-Dixon and Levy commenting on issues pertaining to biological science. While interdisciplinary work is inevitable and necessary, such work requires taking each discipline seriously, and having due regard for the consequences of one's theory. The assumption made about human nature is at its core a political realist one: humans are expected to resort to force and coercion to achieve their goals. There is thus a latent conflation of nature internal with nature external, and both are seen to be anarchic and brutal. With this, nature itself can be seen in threatening terms by people such as Kaplan (1994). The scientific cosmology that denies order in the Other, and which has always underwritten modernity, resurfaces in this environment–conflict literature. The discourse, then, is one of barbaric Southern Others residing in decaying natural environs (over there). It is not surprising, but nevertheless not encouraging, that this has intuitive resonance in the heartlands of modernity.

The environment–conflict literature perpetuates a dualistic understanding of the relationship between humans and the natural world. The relationship is depicted as one in which humans are threatened by nature, or, in some texts, humans are threatening nature. The relationship is always seen to be antagonistic: the exchanges are *threatening*. This recourse to dualism ignores the dialectical understanding of humans as nature rendered self-conscious, which casts environmental security in terms of human health and welfare rather than conflict (see Bookchin 1982).

Conflict, instability and security

The environment–conflict literature talks of conflict in a particular way. Conflict is almost always equated with direct violence. It is used to denote a fundamental Bad which correlates to images of tribal warfare and guerrilla insurgence. This unexplained use of conflict masks the critical assumption that in any conflict violence is the natural outcome, and peaceful resolution the aberration.

Conflict is not necessarily bad, however, nor does it necessarily involve violence of either a direct or a structural kind. Many struggles over resources can be seen to be situations of conflict, yet the vast majority of these are resolved without recourse to violence. Conflict involves struggle between individuals or groups within a society. Many forms of overt struggle – between political parties, sporting teams or academics – do not involve violence. Indeed, discrepancy, disagreement and struggle are inevitable given social diversity. The peaceful resolution of these differences is a basic function of politics and is the essence of civilisation. The failure to resolve these overt struggles peacefully may lead to direct violence occasionally, and to structural injustices more frequently, but violence is not the inevitable outcome of conflict. Indeed, depending on the lens one uses, violence is rarely the outcome of conflict; rather, peaceful conflict is a necessary dialectical process that drives historical change.

This literature uses the word 'instability' in a way very similar to its use of conflict: that is, to denote an undesirable state of affairs. Instability in this context means sudden upheaval and radical change. It equates to a threat to the status quo which, by implication, is the desired state. The environment–conflict literature thus holds to a typically negative conception of security. What is to be secured is the modern world order from the threat of change. Yet, as we have seen, instability and conflict do not necessarily imply change for the worse. Indeed, given that the areas where instability is anticipated are all areas where there are numerous and pervasive injustices and deprivations, instability and change are to be welcomed. If, as it is currently written, environmental security means resisting, avoiding and suppressing change, then it is a vehicle for the continued defence of injustice. Furthermore, given that social changes are inevitable, just as evolution is seemingly natural, suppression of change is ultimately futile. Instead, change should be welcomed and negotiated to ensure that it is non-violent.

Narrowing the issues

The emphasis on conflict occurs at the expense of awareness and understanding of the causes, effects, and solutions to environmental insecurity. This is perhaps a product of the volume of this literature and its intuitive appeal to mainstream international relations. Dabelko and Dabelko are surely right to suggest that 'all issues of environmental degradation should not be forced to fit the matrix of security and conflict' as so often happens in this literature (1995: 8). In so doing, the environment–conflict literature reduces the subject of environmental security, and indeed the broader and more longstanding field of environment and development, to a narrow and ultimately unresolvable set of questions for which international relations scholars are the gatekeepers.

It is desirable, then, to adopt a fuller and more holistic perspective on environmental insecurity. Some of the salient features of this would include appreciation of:

- *cause* – global economic and political processes and the macro-history of modernity;

- *context* – the history behind any particular case, the effects of culture and cultural mixing in any particular case, the biophysical setting, and the ways in which people adapt in ways that do not lead to violence and which may be effective in the short and long term;

• *effects* – declining health and welfare, natural disasters, slow cumulative changes, accidents, and conflict.

In this more holistic perspective conflict is only one of the numerous effects of environmental degradation. Overemphasising conflict therefore precludes recognition of these other effects. Further, when conflict does occur it should be seen as a particular and specific instance, not as proof of the universal inevitability of violence. Finally, a holistic approach implies that environmental security necessitates fundamental reform of the global political economy, and reform of the socially and ecologically degrading features of modernity.

Theory and prophecy

In that Soroos (1994) calls the environment–conflict literature a theoretical argument, it is valid to consider briefly the possibility that this theory may affect a change in social reality consistent with its image. Rogers touches succinctly on this problem:

> There is much evidence that violent conflict occurs because violent conflict is anticipated. The idea of a pre-emptive strike may grow out of basic fight or flight instincts, but it may equally be a self-fulfilling prophecy; the behaviourist product of positivist/Realist assumptions about self interest. (Rogers 1996: 3)

Elliott also warns of the danger that predictions of environmental conflict may become self-fulfilling prophecies (Elliott 1996: 165). In short, in describing a world of 'coming anarchy', the environment–conflict literature helps to reify this world.

In the final analysis, the more telling question about the linkages between environment and conflict is not: is environmental degradation likely to lead to violence? It is not even how might environmental degradation lead to violence? Rather, it is *why are we interested in the linkages* between environmental degradation and violence? In short, why this literature? The thesis that environmental degradation will lead to violence is generally unconvincing and is more a reflection of Northern theoretical and strategic interests than the reality of environmental degradation. This is to say, then, that the first two questions are by and large irrelevant. It is valid at this stage to recall Falk's (1971) suggestion that scarcity will lead to the (potentially violent) defence of power by the already powerful. Given this, the answer to the latter question is that the environment–conflict literature obscures Northern complicity in the generation of the very environmental problems it scripts as threats, and more importantly is a discursive primer to justify the defence of Northern interests in an anticipated era of global environmental change. Thus arises the obsession with only one of the possible effects of environmental degradation (conflict) at the expense of other effects, and at the expense of taking seriously the root causes of the degradation.

6

Policies for Pollution
and the Pollution of Policy

As the concept of environmental security has evolved it has been increasingly used in the United States National Security Strategy and in pronouncements by the United States Departments of Defense and State. These policies warrant examination as they are clear practical manifestations of the concept of environmental security. They reveal the way certain themes of the environmental security literature appeal to policy makers; they allow for the assessment of policies in terms of their likely efficacy; and they offer answers to questions that pervade the concept of environmental security.

The subject of environmental security has been promoted in influential US policy journals such as *International Security, Foreign Affairs* and *Foreign Policy*. Given the leading role of the broader policy community in the United States on the subject of environmental security, and with the high degree of compatibility between their discourses and existing US security discourse, it is not surprising that US foreign policy eventually took environmental security on board. Dabelko and Simmons set the context:

> The number of US government and scholarly endeavors exploring the issues of environment and security, or 'environmental security', is proliferating .... Many senior figures in the Clinton Administration have embraced environment and security ideas. While these ideas have not produced a common policy agenda or focus, numerous rhetorical statements and government initiatives addressing the environment in the context of US security interests have appeared since 1993. (Dabelko and Simmons 1997: 128)

The Clinton administration has created a number of high-level positions to deal with environmental security, including a Senior Director for

Global Environmental Affairs at the National Security Council, a National Intelligence Officer for Global and Multilateral Issues at the National Intelligence Council, a Deputy Under Secretary within the Department of Defense, and an Under Secretary for Global Affairs within the Department of State (Dabelko and Simmons 1997, Thomas 1997).

Recent US statements and initiatives which refer to environmental security can be loosely attributed to the National Security Strategy, the Department of Defense and the Department of State. These three institutions are mutually reinforcing and overlap in their promotion of US security interests. The use of environmental security by the institutions in question is discussed below.

The US National Security Strategy

The US National Security Strategy (NSS) is the most important unclassified statement of US security policy. The NSS has made reference to environmental degradation as a security issue since 1991, and it has figured in subsequent strategies, including the 1998 NSS titled *A National Security Strategy for a New Century* (Clinton 1998). The historic and heroic tone of the 1998 NSS is established in the preface:

> At this moment in history, the United States is called upon to lead – to organize the forces of freedom and progress; to channel the unruly energies of the global economy into positive avenues; and to advance our prosperity, reinforce our democratic ideals and values, and enhance our security. (Clinton 1998: iv)

As it rides shotgun on the stagecoach of freedom and progress, the explicit goal of the National Security Strategy is:

> to ensure the protection of our nation's fundamental and enduring needs: protect the lives and safety of Americans, maintain the sovereignty of the United States with its values, institutions and territory intact, and promote the prosperity and well being of the nation and its people. (p. 5)

Within this context, environmental issues figure as one of a suite of 'new, complex challenges':

> The same forces that bring us closer increase our interdependence, and make us more vulnerable to forces like extreme nationalism, terrorism, crime, environmental damage and the complex flows of trade and investment that know no borders. (p. iii)

We seek a cleaner global environment to protect the health and well-being of our citizens. A deteriorating environment not only threatens public health, it impedes economic growth and can generate tensions that threaten international stability. To the extent that other nations believe they must engage in non-sustainable exploitation of natural resources, our long term prosperity and security are at risk. (p. 5)

Crises are averted – and US preventative diplomacy actively reinforced – through US sustainable development programs that promote voluntary family planning, basic education, environmental protection, democratic governance and the rule of law, and the economic empowerment of private citizens. (p. 8)

Environmental problems are ranked as secondary, albeit important, concerns in the NSS's hierarchy of issues. There are three categories of national interest which indicate the extent to which the Unites States will commit resources to deal with particular problems. The first category, 'Vital Interests', includes the maintenance of territorial integrity, economic well-being, and critical infrastructures, and these are to be defended using military might 'unilaterally and decisively' when necessary (Clinton 1998: 5). The second category, 'Important National Interests', includes issues that do not affect national survival, but do affect national well-being and 'the character of the world in which we live' (Clinton 1998: 5). Issues explicitly mentioned include the flow of refugees and the state of the global environment. In order to protect these important national interests, the US will use its resources 'insofar as the costs and risks are commensurate with the interests at stake' (Clinton 1998: 5). 'Resources' in this sense refers to the integration of foreign assistance, diplomatic, military, and intelligence capabilities. The third and least important category is 'Humanitarian and Other Interests', which includes disaster relief, supporting democratization, promoting development, and promoting human rights (Clinton 1998: 5). So in this schema environmental degradation is a second-tier security issue, and while diplomatic and legal mechanisms have been the preferred avenues for dealing with it thus far, the use of force is not explicitly ruled out in the NSS.

That the environment figures in the NSS leaves no doubt that it is now a security issue, at least for the United States. Yet by virtue of the dominant influence of the United States on world affairs, all nations will need to be familiar with the concept of environmental security if they are to navigate their way successfully in the global political arena. It is therefore important to understand what US policy means when it refers to environmental security.

The NSS sees environmental degradation as a 'threat', indistinguishable from other sources of vulnerability like extreme nationalism, terrorism and crime. Equally, environmental degradation is seen as a 'danger' to US security: 'Environmental threats do not heed national borders and can pose long-term dangers to our security and well-being' (Clinton 1998: 13). The likening of environmental problems to other sources of vulnerability is, as Deudney (1990) suggests, misleading in so far as other problems involve harm being more deliberately imposed by Others from the outside. This leads to inappropriate policy responses.

The NSS selectively interprets environmental problems to include only a few of those aspects that might directly threaten US security interests, such as an influx of environmental refugees, or environmentally induced conflicts. Broader but less tangible problems that might ultimately impact upon the United States, such as declining biodiversity and climate change, are downplayed, while problems exclusively encountered in other places, such as famine and drought, are completely ignored. Exactly how even those dangers that are mentioned threaten the United States is not made clear; these are existential rather than specific threats. This construction of external dangers is of course integral to the delineation of Us from Other and the construction of the nation.

Hence the question *insecurity how?* is never adequately answered in the NSS. At least part of the answer is that the foreign policy community is still fundamentally concerned about environmental degradation restricting 'access to foreign markets' and undermining 'American competitiveness' (both sub-sections of the 1998 NSS). Thus, rather than being the primary concern, environmental insecurity can be read as coda for the meta-concern for declining opportunities for economic growth.

The environmental security perspective of the NSS is strongly influenced by the environment–conflict thesis. This is not surprising given that Kaplan's *Coming Anarchy* 'played a catalytic role in bringing the environment–conflict thesis to the attention of the highest levels of the Clinton Administration and the larger Washington policy community' (Dabelko and Simmons 1997: 136). The NSS is concerned with 'natural resource scarcities' which 'often trigger and exacerbate conflict' (Clinton 1998: 13). This influence is underlined by Eileen Claussen, the Senior Director for Global Environment Affairs at the National Security Council:

'From my perspective, the environment and security relationship builds in part on important linkages between resource scarcity and conflict' (Claussen 1995: 40). Further, President Clinton has referred to the likely outcome of 'terrorism, tension and war' if environmental degradation is not halted (Clinton 1995a: 51). Yet as the previous chapter has argued, despite an extensive literature on the subject it is by no means clear that environmental degradation will result in any increase in violence, particularly between nation-states.

References to 'stability' (and hence instability) in the NSS reflect both a concern for violent conflict (reflecting the influence of realist international relations theory), but also more general political unrest and hence disturbances in the operation of the global market (reflecting the influence of liberal international relations theory). Yet the most frequent and most probable forms of international conflict are not likely to involve direct violence, but will instead take the form of exacerbated diplomatic and trading tensions between North and South, which will arise from the deprivations generated by the US-led global economy, with the tensions of environmental diplomacy superimposed (as Falk suggested as long ago as 1971, see Chapter 4). Such tensions may yet escalate if the United States is careless in its engagement with the South as it seeks to secure the environmental interests it perceives to be important. The NSS can be read as a discursive primer for more cavalier forms of engagement, as suggested by the reference to those 'nations [which] believe they must engage in non-sustainable exploitation of natural resources' as risks to US security and prosperity (Clinton 1998: 5).

That these non-sustainable resource uses are clearly seen as a threat to US security again reflects the influence of inside/outside rationality on the NSS. According to the NSS, 'Environmental threats such as climate change, ozone depletion and the transnational movement of hazardous chemicals and waste directly threaten the health of US citizens' (Clinton 1998: 13). Thus the state is the central referent object of security, and ecological and humanitarian problems that arise outside the US are of secondary importance. This reflects the ongoing problem of viewing environmental degradation from within the national frame of reference, for assessment of the causes (and effects) of environmental degradation defy the state-based classification of world space. In so far as there is some truth to the 'global' nature of environmental degradation, this state-centred approach leads to diminished policy (Dovers 1997). For example, the

NSS has a subsection on 'Promoting Sustainable Development Abroad' as a means to enhance US interests, but much less is said about promoting sustainable development at home, despite the enormous contribution of the US to global environmental change (but see below).

The NSS's discussion of sustainable development is itself confused: 'Environmental and natural resource issues can impede sustainable development efforts and promote regional instability' (Clinton 1998: 33). Hence sustainable development here means sustainable *economic* development; the writers of the NSS are unaware that *ecologically* sustainable development is precisely about these 'environmental and natural resource issues'.

The 1998 NSS is nevertheless better informed with respect to environmental problems than the 1996 and 1997 strategies. The 1995 NSS went so far as to countenance the possibility that there might be competition between nations for 'dwindling reserves of uncontaminated air' (Clinton 1995b: 48). While the context of the 1998 NSS is still very much national security from threats emanating from the outside, there is significantly greater awareness of the measures required to promote environmental security as human security, including increasing aid and promoting family planning and education. The NSS also aims to implement the Programme of Action on population growth developed at the 1995 Cairo Conference, and it seeks to achieve Senate ratification of the Biodiversity Convention, the Law of the Sea Convention and the Convention to Combat Desertification.

Counterbalancing these positive developments, however, is an increasingly (between 1994 and 1998) strong free trade agenda which arguably runs contrary to the goals of environmental security. Economic and energy security still take priority over environmental security in the US strategic vision. Also of concern is the repeated reference to the need to promote 'American values' as a means to enhance 'both our security and prosperity' (Clinton 1998: 2), suggesting not merely an intolerance of difference, but the desire to impose uniformity as a security imperative. Given that the United States is by many indicators the biggest consumer and polluter in the international community, a world shaped in its image would be far from environmentally secure (for data see UNDP 1998). Finally, it is alarming that the United States considers that its nuclear weapons 'serve as a hedge against an uncertain future, a guarantee of our security commitments to allies and a disincentive to those who would contemplate developing or otherwise acquiring their own nuclear weapons' (Clinton 1998: 12).

The US Department of Defense

In 1995, in his annual report to Congress, the US Secretary of Defense asserted that 'environmental security is now an essential part of the US defense mission and a high priority for DOD' (Perry 1995: 1). The involvement of the US Department of Defense (DOD) in environmental security began in 1990 when Senator Sam Nunn, Chair of the Senate Armed Forces Committee, said:

> There is a new and different threat to our national security emerging – the destruction of our environments. The defense establishment has a clear stake in countering this growing threat. I believe that one of our key national security objectives must be to reverse the accelerating pace of environmental destruction around the globe. (Cited in MacDonald 1995: 2)

Nunn uses a particular discursive strategy here, namely the reference to 'global' environmental problems as threats, therefore implicitly justifying military involvement in defence – even though it is less than obvious how the US military might help reverse the accelerating pace of environmental destruction around the globe. As the following chapter argues, there are potential roles for the military with respect to environmental degradation, but none justify continued high levels of expenditure on the military, and few would make a genuine contribution to reducing environmental degradation.

Also in 1990, then Senator Al Gore published a paper calling for a Strategic Environment Initiative (SEI) (Gore 1990). Gore stated that 'the global environment has ... become an issue of national security' and proposed that what was required was 'a mobilization of talent and resources usually reserved only for the purposes of national defense' (Gore 1990: 60, 63). Gore's paper argued that radical changes in the meaning and implementation of development were required if environmental degradation is to be halted. His SEI proposal was consistent with the policy integration idea of sustainable development in that it sought to cut across all policy sectors. He identified energy research and development policy as the sector most urgently requiring reform, seeking to reverse the funding priorities of the US Department of Energy, which in

1990 devoted two thirds of its budget to defence-related programmes and only one fifth to energy research and development (Gore 1990: 66). However, Gore was reluctant to draw on funds from defence to finance environmental policies. This reluctance explains in part why his otherwise commonsense proposals were ultimately reduced to a set of narrow military and foreign policy responses.

Heeding Nunn and Gore, in November 1990 the US Congress allocated US$200 million to the Strategic Environmental Research and Development Program (SERDP), operated by the Department of Defense (Thomas 1997). SERDP's aim is 'to harness some of the resources of the defense establishment ... to confront the massive environmental problems facing our nation and the world today' (DOD 1999). It has four functions: to promote research of relevance to the DOD and the Department of Energy (DOE), enabling them to meet their environmental obligations; to identify outcomes of this research and technologies developed by DOD and DOE which 'would be useful' (read saleable) to other governmental and private organisations; to supply other governmental and private organisations with data and data-handling mechanisms for use in environment-related research and development; and to identify technologies developed by the private sector that might be of use to DOD and DOE (DOD 1999). The implicit function of SERDP seems, therefore, to lie in ensuring that DOD and DOE compliance with environmental regulations is cost-effective, and that any potential marketing possibilities from DOD and DOE research and development are exploited. This commercial function is revealed in a report by then Secretary of Defense William Perry to Congress: 'The Department's [technology] strategy is to ... expedite the use and commercialization of these technologies' (Perry 1995: 3).

In 1993 the Department of Defense upgraded the division responsible for environmental matters, awarding it the official title of Office of the Deputy Under Secretary of Defense (Environmental Security), or DUSD[ES]. Initially, DOD involvement in environmental matters was domestically oriented and not linked to security as such. This involvement began in 1984 with the establishment of the Defense Environmental Restoration Account (Perry 1995). A number of legislative acts progressively forced the DOD and DOE to comply with environmental legislation. The two most important were the 1986 Superfund Amendments and Reauthorization Act, and the Federal Facilities Environmental

Compliance Act of 1992 (Perry 1995). As a result, between 1990 and 1995 the DOD increased its expenditure on environmental programmes from US$1.4 billion to US$5 billion (2 per cent of the total defence budget). Even at this rate the DOD will not comply with current legislation until around 2050 (Thomas 1997). Much of the impetus for the DOD's environmental activities (and SERDP) was not internally driven, therefore, but externally imposed. Thomas (1997) suggests that at the bureaucratic level, the DOD moved to take responsibility for its environmental problems in order to prevent the Environment Protection Agency (EPA) from gaining some leverage over defence policy.

This imposition of compliance is clearly revealed in the first of the DUSD(ES)'s 'overriding and interconnected goals,' which is 'to comply with the law' (DOD 1997). The other three goals are:

To support the military readiness of the US armed forces by ensuring continued access to the air, land and water needed for training and testing;

To improve the quality of life of military personnel and their families by protecting them from environmental, safety, and health hazards and maintaining quality military facilities;

To contribute weapons systems that have improved performance, lower cost, and better environmental characteristics. (DOD 1997)

What is being secured in this interpretation of environmental security is the military readiness of the armed forces rather than the state (as the NSS would have it), let alone the citizens of that state. The threat here is the possibility that environmental degradation might undermine the effectiveness of the US military by limiting access to training areas or by detracting from the health and welfare of military personnel. The nature of the DOD's response is consistent with the reactive and rhetorical position many other sectors and government agencies throughout the world have adopted in response to environmental concerns and laws.

The reference to weapons systems with 'better environmental characteristics' is ambiguous, but in Perry's report he suggests that the DOD is seeking to 'incorporate environmental security considerations into all aspects of weapon system acquisition, maintenance and operations' (Perry 1995: 3). The aim seems to be to factor environmental benefits and costs into weapons systems purchasing. Perry uses phrases like 'where possible' and 'as feasible', which suggests that this is a rhetorical, more than a practical, goal. Indeed, it is difficult to see a secretive weapons negotiation process devoting much attention to the environmental characteristics of the weapon in question. What is likely to be given most attention is the ability of the weapon to *destroy* life rather than to conserve it. This goal of developing 'environmentally benign' weapons is further problematised by the US nuclear arsenal.

Having made these criticisms, one must acknowledge that, if there is to be a military, it might as well be one which seeks to minimise its environmental impacts. If the US DOD has to use 25 million acres of land, and own the 'largest federal archaeological collection in the world', it is a small blessing that it now acknowledges its environmental responsibilities (Perry 1995: 3). However, these responsibilities should be met through substantial action. In the absence of, say, a significant redistribution of funds and personnel, it would seem that the DOD is using environmental security (a term which ideally suits its needs) to promote its (questionable) green credentials and to marginalise the efficacy of scholars and social movements critical of the Pentagon's environmental record (see Renner 1991, Seager 1993, Kuletz 1998).

Looking beyond the borders of the United States, the DUSD(ES) asserts that it has 'a vibrant and growing role in enhancing international environmental security' (cited in Simmons 1996: 132). The Pentagon is seeking to extend its environmental security activities to other regions. Thus:

> The US military's role in environmental protection is manifold: it demonstrates leadership in the US and abroad, helps guarantee access to the air, land and water needed to train US forces and helps promote environmentally sustainable behavior on the part of other militaries around the world.

> DOD's view of 'environmental security' [also comprises] ... understanding where environmental conditions contribute to instability and where the environment fits into the war and peace equation; bringing defense-related concerns to the development of national security; [and] studying how defense components can be used as instruments of US global environmental policy. (Simmons 1996: 132–3)

Thus the Pentagon sees itself as a promoter of sustainability and a leader in environmentally responsible behaviour amongst militaries. This claim is made unselfconsciously and in spite of Renner's observation that the

Pentagon is very likely the largest consumer of energy of any organization in the world and is therefore most likely the world's single largest producer of greenhouse gases (Renner 1991). Further, such claims ignore the point that this damage occurs for no productive outcome other than the dubious need to maintain an extraordinarily large military. The leadership that the US military apparently demonstrates is therefore highly suspect.

When 'access to the air, land and water needed to train US forces' applies to environmental security within the United States, it is tenuous, given that many military training areas have significant environmental contamination and lie adjacent to indigenous peoples' homelands (Seager 1993, Kuletz 1998). But when understood in terms of 'international activities', as it is above, it can be read as a desire to enclose other people's lands for the purpose of military training. On this point it is also worth noting that whilst the DOD may be working towards cleaning up its bases at home, and prides itself on reducing its record of violations of domestic law, there is no similar commitment with respect to cleaning up existing and former US bases abroad. Perry's nine-page report to the President and Congress devotes only seven lines to the issue of overseas bases, as opposed to one and a half pages to 'restoring DOD Facilities' at home. Of these seven lines the salient points are that (my emphasis): 'DOD will *consult* with the host nations on environmental compliance and clean up', and that for the most part 'funding … will be *negotiated* with the host nation' (Perry 1995: 9). So, according to Siegel, 'the official position of the US government is that it is not generally obliged to clean up hazardous wastes at foreign military bases' (Siegel 1996: 16). A genuine commitment from the United States to 'global' environmental security issues would entail a specific and unambiguous programme of action to clean up its overseas bases.

The desire to understand where 'environmental conditions contribute to instability' (see above) is consistent with the NSS, and reflects the influence of the environment–conflict thesis. This confluence between the NSS and the DOD strengthens the links between the military and environmental security. This suggests new reasons to maintain military readiness and so a further reason to forestall budgetary cutbacks. The possibility of a peace dividend is reduced when the impossibility of peace is constantly proven through these discourses of danger. For as long as the emphasis remains on military solutions, then, one can assume that there is a pervasive lack of genuine will to redress environmental insecurity.

The environmental assistance given to other militaries around the world is not given according to need but according to traditional geopolitical dictates. For example, the environment has been a key element of the continuation of NATO beyond the end of the Cold War. Former Secretary General of NATO, Manfred Worner, is particularly revealing, saying that 'no other NATO country, in our traditional division of labor, equals the United States in its global responsibilities' (Worner 1991: 101). The responsibility to which Worner refers is 'to be the purveyor of stability, not only *vis-à-vis* East and Central Europe, but also to the world at large' (102). This can be read as the search for new reasons for old orders, what Worner himself calls a 'shift ... in the rationale for our defense' (102). Worner refers to 'the immense conflict potential that is building up in Third World countries, characterized by ... climate shifts and the prospect of environmental disaster' (103). Thus the environment now figures as part of the rationale for Northern management of global affairs, and serves to justify the maintenance of military power to deal with contingencies. Thus for Dalby 'this NATO understanding of the post-Cold War world is clearly one of the persistence of "Northern" institutions as the core political arrangements from which the rest of the world can be "managed" ... the theme of a select few managing the world's affairs is clear' (Dalby 1999). This is precisely the outcome that those in Southern states feared would result when environmental matters began to be understood as security issues (see, for example, Saad 1995).

The DOD considers that it is 'earning a reputation for strong environmental leadership within NATO'; in the light of the critical reasoning above, therefore, it can be seen to be strongly complicit in the managerial agenda (Perry 1995: 9). The tangible initiatives thus far have focused on Eastern Europe, largely through the auspices of NATO/US confidence-building approaches. The reason for this most likely lies in the discourse of danger that historically has pervaded discussions of Eastern Europe. In contrast, the impoverished South, although scripted in most of the literature as a barbaric Other, has less capacity to threaten the North. Hence despite the efforts of some authors (Ullman and Kaplan, for example) to understand the South as a threat in terms of refugees flows, declining access to valuable resources, and a potential (if vague) disruption to security, these threats are by no means as real as the threat from the usual enemy in Eastern Europe. So there is no action to help the South, and the lack of clear economic returns no doubt compounds the disincentives for doing so. The threat from the South, then, is nothing more than a discursive ploy to keep open the possibility of military intervention in other parts of the world.

As used by the DOD, environmental insecurity is about *realpolitik*. Ethical concerns are absent and 'the good' is understood in a highly parochial, non-universal way. Further, in that military activities create environmental insecurities for people living within the United States, this sense of the good often does not apply to the very people the state claims to protect. More importantly, two thirds of the world's people may well face greater insecurity and deprivation in the future (let alone now), but this is not seen as sufficient cause for substantial action. In this context, environmental security is not about the environment, it is about security; as a concept, it is at its most meaningless and malign.

Efforts to build peace under the rubric of environmental security (and the auspices of the DOD) only focus on those who threaten the capitalist peace. Thus the question must be raised: is the best path to world peace not to arm the South? Would a proliferation of the means of violence expose the ethical interruption that *realpolitik* creates? One would hope not; the logic of violence should not be used to overcome violence. Nevertheless, there are clear limitations to the self-interest rationality prevalent in much of the environmental security literature ('we should act because it is in our interest'). If this remains the strategy of environmental security, and environmental foreign policy more generally, then motivating discourses of danger will have to be constantly recreated, in a disturbingly similar way to that in which threats are sought out by strategic planners to justify militarised national security. Indeed the two logics are wholly interdependent.

The US State Department

The US State Department became formally involved in environmental security in 1996 when Secretary of State Warren Christopher delivered a landmark speech at Stanford University. The Stanford speech is laden with references to the effect of environmental degradation on US interests and security. Christopher identifies two principal reasons why environmental issues must be incorporated into US foreign policy:

First, environmental forces transcend borders and oceans to threaten directly the health, prosperity and jobs of American citizens. Second, addressing natural resource issues is frequently critical to achieving political and economic stability, and to pursuing our strategic goals around the world.

He goes on to add that:

The United States is providing the leadership to promote global peace and prosperity. We must also lead in safeguarding the global environment on which that prosperity and peace ultimately depend. (Chistopher 1996)

This is similar to the claim to global managerialism present in NATO post-Cold War security doctrine. It also misleadingly scripts 'environmental forces' as threats in the same way that the NSS does. The question – *whose security?* (or in this case whose 'peace and prosperity'?) must be asked. The answer is arguably less a universal peace and prosperity and rather more the peace and prosperity of the United States and its allies. Further, the question *insecurity how?* remains unanswered. As with the NSS, the threats are existential, suggesting again the discursive tactic to justify the existing military-managerial approach to global politics.

A notable feature of Christopher's Stanford speech is the way in which it manages to transfer responsibility for environmental problems away from the United States and towards Others via a continued recourse to 'threats to the national interest'. For example:

Across the United States, Americans suffer the consequences of damage to the environment far beyond our borders. Greenhouse gases released around the globe by power plants, automobiles and burning forests affect our health and our climate, potentially causing many billions of dollars in damage from rising sea levels and changing storm patterns.... (Christopher 1996)

Christopher does not mention that 24 per cent of the offending greenhouse gases come from the United States alone, nor that it produced 213,620,000 metric tons of hazardous wastes between 1991 and 1994 (as opposed to 7,000,000 in France and 9,100,000 in Germany) (UNDP 1998).

Christopher indicates the degree to which military power is involved in affecting US strategic goals (my emphasis):

In carrying out America's foreign policy, we will of course use our diplomacy *backed by strong military forces* to meet traditional and continuing threats to our security, as well as to meet new threats…. But we must also contend with the vast new danger posed to our national interests by damage to the environment and resulting global and regional instability. (Christopher 1996)

This passage reveals the linkage of military diplomacy with environmental degradation and instability, suggesting that the military has a potential role to play in managing (anticipated) environmentally induced conflicts, thereby justifying a strong military capability.

The latent economic agenda in US foreign policy is clear in Christopher's speech. For example, the US has an 'enormous stake in consolidating democratic institutions and open markets' (also a strong theme of the NSS). Democracy and free markets are twin pillars of contemporary US foreign policy, yet the two are by no means mutually dependent. An open economy need not respect the rights of its people; indeed, arguably, a government that opens its economy is negligent of its responsibilities to its people. Further, opening the economy to the global market is not necessarily what democracies do. This free market ideology has increasingly saturated US foreign policy (and the NSS) under the guidance of Secretary of State Madeleine Albright and President Bill Clinton.

Christopher's speech unveiled the State Department's Environmental Initiative for the Twenty-first Century, which involves creating alliances between the various divisions of the State Department, forums on key issues and in key regions, and progressively establishing 'environmental opportunity hubs' in key embassies. One of the objectives of these opportunity hubs is to help US businesses sell their environmental technology. The initiative also introduced the Partnership for Environment and Foreign Policy programme, which promotes greater cohesion on environmental issues among the various divisions of the State Department.

A key part of the Environmental Initiative is the production of an annual report, first issued in 1997, a far more informed document than Christopher's early speech. The inside/outside theme is far less evident, although it has by no means disappeared, and there is now some recognition of the US's contribution to global environmental problems. What is also encouraging is a sense of the 'borderless'. For example:

The State Department now operates on the premise that countries sharing common resources share a common future and that neighboring nations are downstream and upwind, not just North and South or East and West, of each other. Threats to a shared forest, a common river, or a seamless coastline are

forcing countries to expand their existing bilateral relationships to include
environmental issues, and to create new regional frameworks to confront and
combat shared environmental challenges. (Department of State 1997)

What is striking here is the presence of an outlook that seems to depart
from the practical geopolitical imagination underlying earlier pronouncements. There is a certain ecological sensibility in the reference to 'downstream and upwind' for example, which indicates either a better
awareness of ecological realities, or a more sophisticated green spin.
Timothy Wirth, the former Under Secretary of State for Global Affairs,
displays a similar ecological sensibility: 'Simply put, the life support
systems of the entire globe are being compromised at a rapid rate – illus-
trating our interdependence with nature and changing our relationship to
the planet' (Wirth 1995: 54).

Finally, although current Secretary of State Madeleine Albright is less
concerned with environmental issues than Christopher, she too displays a
more benign and informed approach to environmental problems. In her
1998 Earth Day speech, for example, security and conflict were mentioned
only once; there was partial recognition of the US responsibilities, and a
welcome humanitarian theme (Albright 1998). All these signs of a shift in
sensibility are encouraging, but more decisive reforms are necessary to
break away from the US's overall interpretation of environmental
security in parochial and strategic terms.

(Re)securing the state

According to Porter, the US approach to environmental security 'clearly
has not led to the militarisation of environmental policy issues' (1995:
222). Similarly, Myers writes that: 'I had never thought I would raise a
cheer for the Pentagon view of life. Hallelujah, it seems there is no limit
to what enlightened people can envision' (Myers 1996: ix–x). What both
fail to recognise is the way in which the US defence and foreign policy
community has narrowed, if not emptied, the concept of environmental
security to justify their position as elite guardians of the national interest.
Dabelko and Simmons (1997: 132) call this a 'classic bureaucratic effort to
retain comparable budgetary outlays and reap public relations benefits',
and Pirages argues that environmental security has 'not revamped foreign
policy and security thinking' in the US (Pirages 1997: 37).

The NSS, DOD and State Department interpret environmental security in a way that maintains the legitimacy of the US government in the face of pressing environmental problems. By deploying a green rhetoric the state makes enough of a token gesture to placate the concerns of the general public and to forestall a crisis of legitimacy. This completely fails to engage with environmental problems themselves, for while environmental insecurity is a product of capitalism, militarism and industrialisation, the approach of these agencies is to deploy 'a complex repertoire of responsibility and crisis-displacement strategies' (Hay 1994: 217).

The US approach to environmental security maintains legitimacy by:

> a combination of symptom amelioration, token gesturism, the 'greening' of legitimating political ideology, and the displacement of the crisis in a variety of different directions: either downward into civil society; or upward onto a global political agenda: or, indeed, sideways in presenting the crisis as another body's (e.g., state's) legitimization problem. (Hay 1994: 221)

Most of these tactics are evident in US environmental security policy discourse. The lethargic effort to clean up domestic contaminated bases but not those abroad is indicative of the 'symptom amelioration' tactic. The 'greening of political ideology' is most clearly manifest in the environment–conflict discourse, which is fundamentally consistent with realist international relations theory. There is little displacement downwards into civil society, but the tactic of displacing problems up to the global level is clear, particularly in Christopher's pronouncements. That this global rhetoric also opens up the possibility of the US as global manager and policeman further enhances the lure of this tactic. Finally, displacement sideways to present environmental degradation as someone else's problem is also clearly apparent in the references to instability and political upheaval which intertwine with the environment–conflict discourse. For the US government, then, environmental security is used to preserve legitimacy, avoid radical reform and distract attention from the contradictions of the modern world for which the US is inextricably responsible. Hay calls such continued strategies of displacement 'dysfunctional long-term tendencies' which in this case make the United States 'a profound threat to global security' (Hay 1994: 227).

All of these approaches to environmental security interpret the environment as a direct or indirect threat to US interests. Talking in terms of threats in this way confuses environmental problems with military problems. This is an inappropriate way to understand environmental problems, particularly given that 'threat' in security discourse is a potent symbol of deliberate and malignant danger to the inside emanating from the outside. In this respect the environment becomes another danger which helps constitute the sense of Us necessary for the popular acceptance of the nation-state. Talking in terms of global threats helps to blur the distinctions between subject and object, and cause and effect, and this obscures US complicity in environmental degradation. This environmental security policy discourse evades the most salient point about national security and environmental degradation: that the country most complicit in 'global' environmental degradation is the United States itself.

Talking in terms of threats is thus a discursive tactic that simultaneously downgrades the interdependence of environmental problems whilst excluding from consideration the role of US businesses, consumers and government in generating environmental problems. Campbell is succinct about this discourse of threats and Others:

> One of the effects of this interpretation has been to reinscribe East–West understandings of global politics in a period of international transformation by suggesting that the 'they' in the East are technologically less sophisticated and ecologically more dangerous than the 'we' in the West. This produces a new boundary that demarcates the 'East' from the 'West'.... But environmental danger can also be figured in a manner that challenges traditional forms of identity inscribed in the capitalist economy of the 'West'. As a discourse of danger which results in disciplinary strategies that are deterritorialized, involve communal cooperation, and refigure economic relationships, the environment can serve to enframe a different reading of 'reasoning man' than that associated with the subjectivities of liberal capitalism, thereby making it more unstable and undecidable than anticommunism. (Campbell 1992: 197)

It is precisely these implications of deterritorialization, communal cooperation and refiguring economies that threaten the US security elite, and so are denied and excluded in their environmental security pronouncements.

Another failing of the threat discourse is that it focuses attention on issues 'only when crises are imminent, by which time it is often too late for effective interventions and corrective measures' (Dabelko and Simmons 1997: 142). This is another example of what Prins calls the environmental Catch-22: by the time environmental problems are unambiguously overt it is too late to rectify them; on the other hand, unless the problems are immediately pressing there is insufficient motivation to result in action by mainstream political institutions (Prins 1990). Thus the particular state- and military-centred interpretation of environmental security by the US policy community ignores a telling implication of environmental problems for politics: that long-term and fundamental reforms are required to address the underlying structural causes of environmental degradation.

This presentation of environmental problems as threats rests on a recurrent conflation of threat with risk. Environmental security in this sense represents the state's particular highly politicised assessment of risk rather than any scientific account of the actual risks. There is little correlation between the two; most often the way states respond to environmental problems is conditioned by political factors more than informed risk assessments. Certainly the US government's assessment of risks is far less a matter of credible scientific assessment and far more a matter of the politics of identity and Otherness. The challenge, according to Hay, is to continue to provide informed risk assessments, and 'to expose the distortions imposed by the state's own consequence-risk calculus' (Hay 1994: 226). This chapter has sought to expose such distortions in US policy.

Beneath current US initiatives and pronouncements on environmental security lies a resistance to meaningful change and a defence of the status quo. As Dalby notes, 'in so far as security is premised on maintaining the status quo it runs counter to the changes needed to alleviate many environmental and economic problems because it is precisely the status quo that has produced the problems' (Dalby 1994: 33). The US government's response to environmental security is not the new foreign and security policies we might have expected to flow from the concept; instead, it has responded with the usual approach to foreign policy based on inside/outside rationality. For the US, environmental security is about securing the very lifestyles and institutions that degrade the environment against the risks associated with this same degradation. This is a paradox lost on most, and a dangerous and counterproductive outcome which cannot be ignored by any proponent of environmental security. Thus President Bush's comment at Rio in 1992 – that the lifestyle of the US is not negotiable – still holds true.

Thus far US environmental security policy has done little to help minimise the causes of environmental insecurity, indeed it seems fundamentally implicated in their perpetuation. It does not recognise that fundamental long-term changes in the structure of the global political economy are required; nor does it recognise that, if any single country needs to implement this reform, it is the US itself. Instead, it holds to a singular belief that the best way to secure against threatening Others is to prepare for war; the irony in this strategy of securing against violence by advocating violence is well known. But, as we shall see in the following chapter, preparing for war is a significant cause of the very environmental degradation the US military finds so threatening, and so the outcome of these policies is a continued spiralling downwards of the interrelated problems of direct violence, structural violence and environmental insecurity.

Weighed against these negative features of US environmental security policy are two principal positive outcomes. First, that environmental concerns now figure in US national security reasoning suggests that the policy community is at least attentive to environmental concerns, even if it interprets them in overly narrowly and parochial ways. More importantly – indeed, it is perhaps the most valuable function of the concept – environmental security creates a basis for dialogue between the Green movement and national security planners. The incorporation of environmental security into US foreign policy therefore serves an extremely important epistemic function which offers the possibility of a more benign and environmentally effective US foreign policy.

The second positive aspect of US environmental security policy is that there is a discernible shift in both the NSS and the pronouncements of the State Department towards a more sensitive understanding of environmental problems. Between 1996 and 1998 the NSS dropped a number of references to environmental degradation as a threat, and has downplayed the possibility of environmental degradation leading to violent conflicts. More importantly, the NSS now recognises the need for non-coercive forms of diplomacy and the ratification of existing international conventions and treaties. Over the same short period the State Department has also developed a more sophisticated approach to environmental problems, and has downplayed the inside/outside theme which traditionally has characterised foreign policy. There remains a danger, however, that the self-congratulatory, vague and militaristic interpretation of environmental security by the Pentagon will counteract these small positive gains made by the NSS and the State Department.

The future utility of the concept of environmental security in American foreign policy is thus still unclear, as is the future contribution of the United States to genuine global peace and security. What is clear, however, is that the deployment of environmental security in US foreign policy intertwines the future of the concept with the future of the planet. This analysis of US environmental security policy has shown that there are real dangers in linking environmental security to the concept of national security. The most pressing danger is that the military and security elite will appropriate the concept to advocate business as usual. Yet despite the fundamental problems that arise from associating environmental security with national security, the concept should not be completely divorced from the national referent. There are at least some valid connections between environmental degradation and the national interest, although the implications of making these connections need to be carefully considered. The issue is one of degree and emphasis. In short, while there is no doubt that environmental security is highly problematic when viewed solely in national terms, there is equally no doubt that the nation-state has an important role to play in acting for the betterment of the environment and the environmentally insecure, because the nation-state is not likely soon to disappear from the political landscape. The concept of environmental security therefore needs to be understood in such a way that non-national – particularly human – referents take precedence over the national referent. In such a conceptualisation, national policy becomes the means to secure *people* rather than the means to secure the state.

7

The Biggest of Institutional Challenges
The Military

A significant subset of the literature on environmental security considers the linkages between the traditional agents of security – the military – and the environment. Because in most countries the military is integral to security policy, talking about environmental security frequently leads *ipso facto* to consideration of the role of the military (defined here as armed forces, their bureaucracies and the military-industrial complex: that is, the entire sector devoted to the conduct of war). The military is an immensely expensive and politically powerful institution, justified solely in the name of national security.

The landmark *Our Common Future* report from the World Commission on Environment and Development referred to the 'institutional challenge' of sustainable development, which is to consider the ecological dimensions of all policies on all issues and all national and international institutions (WCED 1987). While for the most part, in most places, this challenge remains unanswered, the one policy sector that is most immune from this challenge is defence. This is not surprising, since environmental concerns seem to be anathema to the serious business of defence and security. Yet defence, so often one of the top five areas of national spending, should be a high priority for the institutional challenge. Indeed, when this fiscal dimension is considered along with the historical and cultural nature of the military, it is arguably the biggest such challenge.

This chapter measures up the challenge first by looking at the impact of warfare on the environment, and the impacts that result from preparation for warfare (the day-to-day business of the military). It then directly addresses the institutional challenge by exploring the potential for militaries to assist in the recovery and protection of the environment. This complex and contentious issue has been accorded relatively little scholarly attention thus far, and so receives most attention in this chapter. A case study is presented of the potential for Australia's military forces to assist with environmental recovery and protection.

War and the environment

Warfare leads to environmental degradation, and it has done throughout history. In recent times the use of defoliants in Vietnam and the burning of oil wells in Kuwait have further demonstrated that war has significant environmental consequences (Westing 1976, Ramachandran 1991). These consequences are manifest long after fighting has ended (Seager 1993). Because warfare is precisely about the destruction of life, it is axiomatic that it also damages the environment.

Environmental degradation can be an unintended outcome of war, as in the case of the nuclear winter that would be the likely result of a nuclear war. The environment can also be deliberately manipulated as a military strategy. There is more to this than targeting certain facilities (such as nuclear power plants, dams and oil pipelines) to degrade an opponent's operational environment and natural capital. The deliberate destruction or manipulation of the environment has more 'elegant' forms as well (Westing 1997: 145). Among these, the release of harmful micro-organisms is one likely strategy; indeed, this is the function of biological weapons which might disperse, for example, the anthrax virus. Other forms of environmental manipulation for the purposes of warfare include seeding clouds to induce rainfall, and the dispersal of unspecified substances into the troposphere to hamper the effectiveness of radar (Westing 1997). Westing goes as far as to imagine that 'it may become possible to temporarily disrupt the ozone layer above enemy territory for the purpose of permitting injurious levels of ultraviolet radiation to reach the ground' (Westing 1997: 147).

There is a considerable amount of literature that addresses the international agreements and cultural norms required to limit degradation of the environment in times of war and not-war (for example, Lorenz 1994, Westing 1984, 1988a). The partial Test Ban Treaty which sought to minimise fallout from atmospheric nuclear tests is an early example of efforts to reduce the environmental impacts of military activity. Other treaties include the Outer Space Treaty, the Sea-bed Treaty, the

Biological Weapons Convention, the Threshold Test Ban Treaty and the Environmental Modification Convention. In that all rules of military engagement are for the most part ineffective, given that war is far from a civilised and organised event, this approach is perhaps less useful than strategies to address the broader problem of warfare itself.

Preparing for war and the environment

In addition to having significant environmental impacts in times of war, military activities in periods of not-war are also environmentally degrading. When not fighting wars, militaries are preparing to fight the next war. There is thus a state of continuous low-intensity warfare with cumulative environmental impacts, including the use and degradation of land, the pollution and use of airspace, the use of energy and material resources, and the generation of toxic wastes (Renner 1991).

Modern armed forces require large amounts of land for training. For example, the US Department of Defense controls 25 million acres of land (Perry 1995) and the Australian Department of Defence controls 3.6 million hectares (8.9m acres) (making it the largest land holder of any Commonwealth government department) (Cooksey 1988). Advances in weapons technology (bigger impacts and the shrinking of space) increase the military's demand for land. The irony of military land use is that 'in the name of defending a nation's territorial integrity ... larger and larger areas are given over to the armed forces, effectively withdrawing them from public access' (Renner 1991: 134).

Some militaries use the land of other countries for training. For example, in the 1980s the US military was the largest holder of agricultural land in the Philippines (Renner 1991: 135). Seager estimates that there are more than 3,000 military bases located on foreign soil, and that as a rule the environmental impacts of militaries operating on foreign soil are worse than at domestic locations (1993: 57).

Weapons testing is a major cause of land degradation. In Australia, for example, the Port Wakefield weapons testing area cannot be used for alternative purposes as a result of unexploded ordinance accumulated over some 50 years of testing (Social and Ecological Assessment Pty Ltd 1985). Military contamination of land is most extreme where nuclear weapons have been involved. The US nuclear weapons programme was conducted in 34 states and covered 2.4 million acres of land; clean-up costs are expected to be US$200–300 billion (Dycus 1996: 5). In Australia, British nuclear weapons tests at Maralinga and the Monte Bello Islands have rendered these areas uninhabitable (DPIE 1990). Nuclear tests have been carried out at seven sites in the South Pacific, making four islands completely uninhabitable and causing above average cancer levels in residents of the Marshall Islands (Seager, 1995, Siwatibau and Williams 1982).

The manufacture and storage of nuclear and chemical weapons, and the storage and improper disposal of fuel, paints and solvents, generates significant amounts of toxic waste on military sites. The former Soviet Union, for example, has dumped up to 17,000 containers of nuclear waste and up to 21 nuclear reactors into the Barents and Kara seas (Heininen 1994: 156); and the US military generates more toxins than the top five US chemical companies combined (Renner 1991: 143). Seager lists 26 US military bases with significant toxic hazards, and cites a clean-up figure of US$400 billion (1993: 34–5). Ackerman notes that there are some 14,000 US Army, Navy and Air Force sites which require some degree of clean-up (1990: 37); later estimates put this figure at 25,000 potentially contaminated sites (Siegel 1996: 15). Indeed, 'if every military-blighted site around the world were marked on a map with red tack-pins, the earth would look as though it had measles' (Seager 1993: 14).

The use of airspace by military aircraft is a significant environmental hazard. Renner notes that 'an F-18 jet flying at supersonic speed for 10 minutes ... can 'boom' an area of more than 5,000 square kilometres' (1991: 136). The intense noise generated by military aircraft impacts negatively on human health and ecosystem integrity. Flight training in the US is conducted on the territories of 14 Native American nations, which suggests that not all people are secured when national security is procured through the military. Indeed, indigenous people frequently suffer from military activity; to note but one example, during the Kangaroo 95 military exercises held in Northern Australia, a Leopard tank drove through, and damaged, an Aboriginal sacred site.

Militaries use massive amounts of energy and other resources. Early in the 1990s, the worldwide use of aluminium, copper, nickel and platinum for military purposes exceeded the combined demand for these materials in all the industrialising countries (Renner 1991: 140). One quarter of all the world's jet fuel is consumed by military aircraft (Renner 1991: 137). Renner figures that the US military-industrial complex may be responsible for at least 10 per cent of total US carbon dioxide emissions, which makes the DOD responsible for some 2–3 per cent of total global emissions (Renner 1991: 139). The DOD therefore emits more carbon dioxide than all of Canada, or more than all of Australia, Finland, Sweden and New Zealand combined (after UNDP 1998). A 1997 release from the Australian Ministry for Defence gave the following annual fuel costs for Australia's various weapons platforms: F-111 aircraft – A$8 million; F/A-18 aircraft – A$19 million; DDG destroyers – A$19 million; and FFG frigates – A$15 million (Jennings 1997). The total annual fuel bill for operating Australia's eight major weapons platforms in 1997 was A$48.6 million; to compare, Federal funding for renewable energy research and development in 1998 was A$16 million (Parer 1998).

The environmental legacy of military activities works in other less direct ways as well. The social impact of military bases is important. Both Enloe (1990) and Seager (1993) have documented the extremely disruptive effects of military bases on local communities. These effects are more pronounced in industrialising countries and in places with non-Western cultures. Seager argues that there are strong linkages between a foreign military presence, exploitative prostitution, socio-economic segregation and the deterioration of public safety and the environment. The generation of poverty by undermining traditional livelihoods and supplanting them with a largely prostitution-based economy, as in the Philippines for example, has significant ramifications for ecological and social sustainability in these areas. The other great (and perhaps most pervasive) impact of militaries everywhere is the dissemination of a militarised masculinity which propagates itself in a culture that glorifies violence (Enloe 1990).

A well-known negative aspect of military activity is that it displaces expenditure on programmes to improve social and ecological sustainability. As US President Eisenhower noted: 'every gun that is made, every warship fired, signifies in the final sense a theft from those who hunger and are not fed, those who are cold and not clothed'. This can be revealed by expressing military spending as a percentage of government expenditure on health and education. For example in the United States (1991) military expenditure was equivalent to 46 per cent of all expenditure directed towards meeting the health and education needs of US citizens (UNDP 1998). Comparable figures are (1991): Myanmar 222 per cent, the Russian Federation 132 per cent, Bangladesh 41 per cent, France 29 per cent, Guyana 21 per cent and Australia 24 per cent (UNDP 1998). For the industrialised countries military expenditure far exceeds official development assistance (ODA) to industrialising countries. In 1995 the United States disbursed the equivalent of only 3 per cent of its defence budget on ODA; comparable figures are: Australia 14 per cent, France 18 per cent, Canada 23 per cent and Japan 29 per cent (UNDP 1998). In this sense, environmental security implies redirecting military expenditure.

In short, the world's militaries are most probably the single largest institutional source of environmental degradation. This raises serious questions about the possibility of militaries having a positive role in environmental protection and recovery.

Meeting the challenge

Because the military is at present the principal provider of national security, understanding environmental degradation as a security issue implies a role for the military beyond being involved in (questionably) environmentally induced conflicts. Besides being required to take care of its own environmental impacts, there are a number of potential roles for the military: it can assist with the enforcement of environmental standards; it can, along with intelligence agencies, monitor and collect information about environmental degradation; and it can be deployed in broader non-coercive roles to help with environmental conservation and restoration.

Coercive roles

Given that traditionally militaries have used force to achieve a desired outcome, it is inevitable that some authors have advocated military enforcement of certain environmental goals. For example, Julian Oswald (former First Sea Lord of the United Kingdom) envisions a 'traditional coercive task' for militaries, including enforcement of international law at sea (1993: 129). The possibility of a UN-sanctioned green police force (like that of the peacekeeping force) also implies a coercive role for militaries (Schrijver 1989).

There are numerous military-to-military programmes which involve transfers of technology and training for civil and environmental policing activities. For example, the US Security Assistance Program has been involved in helping some African countries to manage the problem of illegal fish and wildlife poaching (Butts 1994). The Pacific Patrol Boat Programme operated by the Australian Navy performs a similar function in the South Pacific (Bergin 1994). These programmes operate in the grey zone between military and non-military threats to security, yet they nevertheless entail responding with military means. This can lead to a paramilitarisation of environmental regulation.

These coercive roles are a reactive and short-term response that does not deal directly with the underlying causes of environmental degradation. Byers explores the possibility of a coercive role for the military in biodiversity protection, and concludes that 'shooting poachers and illegal loggers is [not] a good idea ... as usual with violent means, the means may corrupt and compromise the ends' (Byers 1994: 125). Byers's most persuasive point is that locally derived solutions will always be more effective and long-lasting than externally imposed ones, particularly when those impositions involve the use of force. Thus he argues that 'a long-term solution requires ecologically sustainable economic alternatives for local people' (Byers 1994: 125). Aside from its being an ineffective policy response, the greatest problem with the use of military power to force environmental compliance is the way it enables the military to colonise environmental issues. It also justifies the maintenance of armed forces. If the concept of environmental security induces the appropriation of the environmental agenda in the way that it already has in the United States (as discussed in the previous chapter), then actively encouraging coercive military engagement with environmental problems is likely to lead to ecototalitarianism. Military force will not help to overcome environmental insecurity.

Intelligence and surveillance

A potentially more benign suggestion is to use military and intelligence agencies to assist with analysis, assessment and monitoring of environmental problems. There have been a number of environment-related programmes involving the US Department of Defense and intelligence agencies. These are for the most part reconnaissance missions. For example, in 1993 the US Navy allowed non-military scientists to use the classified Integrated Undersea Surveillance System to track whales in the Western North Atlantic ocean (Thomas 1997). The extension beyond its military application and into civilian use of the Global Positioning System has also had significant benefits for environmental science: in 1995 the US declassified and released for public scrutiny 800,000 of its earliest satellite photographs – largely for the purposes of environmental monitoring (Thomas 1997). In Australia, the work of the Navy Hydrographer in charting the coastline is arguably a function which assists in environmental monitoring and assessment.

Intelligence agencies are important in this information-gathering process. The Director of the US Central Intelligence Agency talks about 'environmental intelligence', and is extremely revealing as to its purposes:

> Much of the work that now falls under the environmental label used to be done under other names – geography, resource issues, or research. For example, we have long used satellite imagery to estimate crop size in North Korea and elsewhere. This allowed us to forecast shortages that might lead to instability and to determine the amount of agricultural production a nation would need to import – information valuable to the US Department of Agriculture and to America's farmers. We have also tracked world availability of natural resources, such as oil, gas, and minerals.... Environmental intelligence will also be a part of our support to economic policymakers. They need to know, for example, whether or not foreign competitors are gaining a competitive advantage over American business by ignoring environmental regulations. (Deutch 1997: 114)

If we decipher the conflation of foci with function, Deutch is admitting that the US uses its satellites to monitor global agricultural production and then to modify domestic output and target markets accordingly. This makes a further mockery of the idea of a 'level playing field' in global trade and the attendant neoliberal abstraction that all rational economic actors have equal access to information in the market. The irony is that the same technology that confers this advantage will be used to enforce the environmental standards that are only tenable in industrialised economies. In effect, the US presses its information advantage for the purposes of profit whilst ensuring that it maintains authority in the affairs of other states under the ambit of environmental monitoring. Deutch understands non-compliance to be important only in so far as competitors might gain an 'advantage', which reinforces the point that environmental intelligence for the US is wholly subservient to the main function of intelligence in the post-Cold War globalising economy – that of maintaining comparative advantage.

The CIA is working with the EPA to combat black market trade in ozone-depleting chlorofluorocarbons, and the US intelligence community also monitors illegal driftnet fishing (Dabelko and Simmons 1997). A particularly interesting programme is the Global Fiducial Data

Program which uses high resolution spy satellites to collect data about environmental change (Thomas 1997). A key feature of this programme, coordinated by the CIA and administered by the National Reconnaissance Office, is that the data remain secret in order to conceal the US's reconnaissance capabilities (Deibert 1996, Thomas 1997). This enclosure of information renders it virtually useless for the peaceful resolution of environmental problems. Instead, it gives the US a privileged and exclusive monopoly of knowledge, the use of which will always be suspicious. Thomas (1997) suggests that most of these dual-use strategies are secrecy-preserving and that this secrecy will serve more to protect the security establishment than to advance environmental interests. If information is to be contributed by military and intelligence agencies, it must remain accessible to all to have a positive environmental outcome.

Despite these problems, intelligence agencies arguably do have a mandate to think about long-term threats to environmental security (however conceived) (Dalby 1995). For Dalby, positive contributions might involve monitoring the state of renewable energy technologies and analysing evidence about environmental change, possibly using 'worst-case' reasoning (which would be consistent with the precautionary principle). He suggests that the privileged position of intelligence analysts in the security policy community might enable them to promote positive and long-term policies. At the heart of these suggestions is a programme to change the practice of national security. This subject of constructive engagement with the security establishment is fraught with danger and there are no easy answers. The later part of this chapter tackles this difficult subject.

Civil defence and non-core roles
Militaries often have civil defence functions, such as disaster relief and the provision of engineering, medical, transport and logistical services to the broader community (Stern 1995). It could also be argued that the US Army Corps of Engineers makes a positive contribution to environmental protection by building water-resource infrastructure. In Australia, the most significant funding and research conducted on hazards and emergency management occurs under the auspices of the Department of Defence. These civil defence activities, because they are non-coercive and have little to offer the military in terms of training, could be described as non-military functions.

These civil defence functions serve as an important precedent for a third kind of positive contribution from the military – the application of the military to non-military environmental tasks. Militaries generally have some unique characteristics that make them useful for dealing with environmental problems: they are well-organised, large-scale, well-resourced, and located in most areas of most countries (Butts 1994: 84). From a broad interpretation of national security which understands environmental degradation to be a risk to national security (as discussed in Chapter 4), it is possible to argue that there is indeed good reason to involve the military in environmental protection and restoration. This book generally supports this argument, but some important caveats are necessary. First, the military should participate in non-coercive ways; second, it should not operate beyond its own nation's borders; third, any activity should be unclassified, including any information collected. This proposition will now be grounded by applying it to Australian defence policy.

A positive role? The case of Australia

The Australian Defence Mission is 'to promote the security of Australia, and to protect its people and interests' (Commonwealth of Australia 1996). As discussed in Chapter 4, environmental degradation does threaten Australia's security, people and interests in important ways. A broad interpretation of the Defence Mission therefore suggests that the Australian Defence Force's contribution to society has been overly narrow, and that there is a need to redefine the role of the military in the light of widespread domestic environmental degradation. As environmental degradation increases, a policy of expanding the military's involvement in environmental protection and restoration becomes increasingly relevant.

It is in Northern Australia that there is the greatest potential for a significant contribution from the Australian Defence Forces to environmental protection and restoration. Northern Australia is defined as the area between Cairns and Broome. This is the area of direct military interest for current Australian defence policy; however, it is also of crucial importance for environmental, economic, social and cultural security. Northern Australia contains vast tracts of unique, relatively undamaged ecosystems vital to Australia's natural heritage. Preserving the ecological integrity of the region would be environmental security in its purest interpretation. The region is also vital to Australia's heritage as it is an area where Aboriginal culture remains vibrant.

The environment of the region is at risk, and many of these risks have already materialised (unlike highly subjective military risks). The outbreak of the papaya fruit fly in 1996 was one of many ecological invasions which have had negative environmental (and economic) consequences. Northern Australia is a zone of transboundary environmental traffic. The region is a major and the most proximate gateway between Australia and Asia and it has a large volume of people, flora and fauna flowing across its borders. With this volume of traffic, both official and unofficial, comes the importation of harmful biological organisms. Although this is also true of all Australian airports and ports, Northern Australia is the most problematic of these high-risk areas as the coastline is over 6,000 kilometres long and most of it is sparsely populated and has little infrastructure. This makes adequate coverage of the area, for whatever purpose, exceedingly difficult. In terms of biological organisms, the smuggling of native fauna, illegal immigration, and drug trafficking, there is currently no comprehensive monitoring system in place. Even in military security terms, despite being the focus of extensive effort, Northern Australia continues to be virtually indefensible against low-intensity threats (Evans 1990).

Australian defence policy currently adopts a layered approach (defence in depth) to the surveillance of the sea–air barrier and inshore areas of Northern Australia (Commonwealth of Australia 1994). At present, ADF activities in Northern Australia do little for the environmental security of the region, but there is much potential for a convergence of activities to address these not dissimilar interests. The best strategy would be a multipurpose, coordinated and comprehensive surveillance and monitoring system. Such a system would integrate civilian and military communication, transport, and aerial infrastructure, in conjunction with local communities, to look for signs of environmental disturbances such as new species of weeds and wildlife smuggling. This would be impossible in the short term without the involvement of the ADF. Involvement in a comprehensive, wide-area surveillance network would be an ideal first step towards an environmental component to the ADF's corporate goal. Any information gathered by such a network must be made publicly available.

As with any challenge to the status quo, resistance to the proposal to involve the military in environmental action can be expected. In a related exploration of resistance to change, Cheeseman identifies two likely sources of opposition to this proposal (Cheeseman 1995). The first is of an ideological nature, namely that Australian defence discourse is incapable of considering alternative conceptions of security as these challenge state authority and the assumption of the need for military might in an (uncritically presumed) anarchic world. Thus an ideological shift is required. The second source of opposition is related. Alternative security policies would make explicit the recognition of the multi-dimensional nature of security in the post-Cold War world. This would radically change the business of the ADF, and fundamentally challenge the expertise and authority of existing defence policy makers (Cheeseman 1995). Thus the suggestion that the Australian defence establishment should add environmental protection and restoration to its core agenda will meet with substantial ideologically and pragmatically driven resistance. Overcoming this resistance will require the development of detailed proposals that promote environmental objectives at the same time as offering some return to the ADF for its involvement (most probably in the form of improved public relations, but this should not be given freely). Overcoming this resistance will also require continued challenging of the meaning and practice of security.

Environmental groups may also resist the prospect of military involvement in environmental management – with good reason, given the experience in the US thus far, and given the extensive environmental damage militaries create. These concerns will be discussed below. Here it is necessary to note that whatever environmental programmes the military might be involved in, these must be practical, domestic, non-coercive, and carefully steered by environmental groups and other stakeholders. Given these conditions, there is potential for the Australian military to engage in environmental protection and restoration in a useful way. Nevertheless there are many risks with such a policy.

Risks, risks, and some opportunities

Arguments against military involvement in environmental issues come from two vastly different perspectives. From the traditional security camp there is resistance to any expansion of military activity lest it undermine the ability to wage war. According to Cohn (1996), Republicans in the

US Congress and military leaders are opposed to non-military operations as these divert time and resources away from core functions. The argument from conservative security planners is that armed forces sacrifice operational readiness by being involved in non-traditional activities such as environmental protection (Dabelko and Simmons 1997: 138). This argument, seeking to preserve the sanctity of national security and the military, may in itself incline one to believe that there must be at least some merit in the proposal that militaries should be involved in environmental protection and restoration.

The second argument against military involvement in these activities is less easy to dismiss. For most environmentalists, the prospect of military involvement in environmental protection and restoration triggers an immediate sense of unease. This is in part due to the intuitive baggage that accompanies environmental sensibility, which holds to values such as anti-authoritarianism, cooperation, social justice and peace, all of which are the antithesis of military culture and practice. Further, given the extensive environmental damage wrought by military activity, it is valid to argue that 'the military must be addressed as a cause and not a cure of global environmental problems', and that 'in the long run, the industrial-military complex must be dismantled ... this is the *sine qua non* for effectively dealing with the entire global environmental crisis' (Finger 1991: 225). This is undoubtedly true in principle.

A further danger in arguing for (even non-coercive) military involvement is that it may justify the continued existence of the military and intelligence agencies by giving them a *mission* (Deibert 1996). This seems borne out in Deutch's observation that applying intelligence collection assets to environmental issues is relatively cheap and easy; therefore the environment serves as a further justification for traditional military and intelligence functions (Deutch 1997). Thus military and intelligence agency involvement in environmental protection and restoration may well be a pragmatic strategy designed to maintain current levels of funding for defence; a bureaucratic tactic designed to hedge against payment of the post-Cold War peace dividend (Finger 1991, Dabelko and Simmons 1997).

While these are all extremely valid concerns with which this book has much empathy, they are all negative in their implications, advocating a return to the situation that prevailed before the concept of environmental security emerged. But if this concept is to have any positive effect, the question of what to do with the military must be addressed, not ignored. Westing's question – 'how can the need for a military sector be reduced?' – is therefore salient (Westing 1988b: 156). Renner, too, is concerned that 'a lasting peace cannot be built without dealing with the remnants of the war system' (1994: 12). Eckersley also supports this view:

> [S]imply documenting and censuring the multiple ecological sins of the military ... avoids the more difficult question of determining whether the military has any legitimate role in promoting national and global environmental protection. Perhaps some of the fog surrounding the concept of environmental security might lift with a tighter clarification of the proper role of the military.... (Eckersley 1996: 143)

In this respect, Finger's reference to 'the long run' (see above) ignores the more immediate and pragmatic question of what to do in the short term. It is precisely this need for a short-term strategy that careful and controlled military involvement in environmental restoration and protection might be able to satisfy.

The present response to the problem of what to do with the military takes two forms. First, it is simply ignored. Second, there is a focus on conversion, which is both a 'reallocation of resources from the military to civilian purposes' (Luckham 1987: 40), and 'a political and institutional transformation' (Renner 1990: 157). While ignoring the issue obviously contributes nothing to the problem, the latter approach has produced negligible results. Conversion is a prescription for change based on high ideals rather than practicality. It does not seriously address the power of the military to resist change.

The contention of this book, then, is that a policy to involve the military in environmental protection and restoration, although fraught with problems, is an achievable and relatively non-threatening way of overcoming this sector's inertia. Involving the military should be seen as a transitional step towards overcoming the structural causes of environmental degradation; to put it another way, it is a pre-conversion conversion. A danger of this policy proposal is that the military may colonise the environmental agenda; this can be averted by involving a diverse array of interests (all stakeholders) in steering its implementation.

The danger of the military pragmatically using environmental security to maintain relevance and legitimacy (as the US Department of Defense has done) is a legitimate and realised concern, but it is similarly pragmatic to involve the military given that environmental degradation is a challenge to *all* institutions. Environmental security offers an opportunity for biophysical scientists to gain assistance and resources, and an opportunity for peace activists to 'grasp in reality what had for so long merely been a quaint [metaphor] in the minds of utopians – a chance to beat swords into plowshares' (Deibert 1996: 29). A further consideration is that any state that acts first can induce a flow-on by setting an example that other militaries may follow (Maddock 1995, Soroos 1994). If the US were to take such a lead, others would be sure to follow. Alternatively, a coalition of middle powers might, by their example, prove the possibility of a shift in military purpose and culture. Finally, there is something to be said for involving the military in environmental protection and restoration because it is the most autonomous of government institutions, and hence the most difficult of all institutions to modify.

There is a paradox here in that the more important the military-industrial complex, the more likely the nation-state is to protect its military rather than the biosphere (Finger 1991: 224). Involving the military in environmental issues is thus least likely to be successful in those places where its transformation is most necessary. But, by the same token, the most resistant to change will be the most resistant to *any* initiative for change. While Finger's point is well taken, therefore, it does not suggest an alternative option for reform of the military. The option proposed here seems more probable and plausible than many others, particularly given a high level of public concern about environmental problems in many countries. Indeed, given the tendency of people to profess concern but actually do little except expect government to take control, a policy to involve the military may well be extremely popular.

Such a policy has relevance in most countries, but should not be seen to be universally applicable. The desired approach to military involvement in environmental protection and restoration is to operate on a case-by-case, country-by-country basis. Military involvement would be one thing in a totalitarian state, for example, but quite another in a liberal-democratic middle power such as Australia, or in a superpower such as the United States. Yet even in a totalitarian state characterised by military dominance of public life it is possible that little would be lost were the military to engage in environmental protection and restoration; and that much might be gained if this were to result in even a slight shift in culture or social dynamics away from repression. The crucial consideration in this proposal is not the potential environmental contribution a military can make, as it will almost always be a better environmental outcome if militaries were disbanded and resources redirected to social and environmental policies. The crucial gain comes from shifting an otherwise rigid, autonomous and wasteful institution and culture.

In sum, the institutional challenge of sustainability requires large and fundamental structural changes in all policy sectors, and so an open mind is needed when considering what each institution – including, and perhaps most importantly, the military – has to offer. Provided the military can be encouraged to participate (and here the notion of environmental security may help), and provided this participation is conducted in a practically and morally acceptable manner, military involvement in environmental protection and restoration is a significant step towards structural change. To reiterate, vital caveats are that any such military programme must seek a positive environmental outcome, be of a noncoercive nature, be restricted to action within the country concerned, and be implemented with the involvement of Green groups and local stakeholders. The fundamental goal of a policy to involve the military in environmental protection and restoration is not the continuation of the security establishment but, on the contrary, its gradual conversion. This, then, is one implication of the concept of environmental security that may, in the long term, serve the interests of peace and human security.

That the US military has thus far employed the concept of environmental security in such a way as to maintain its privileged position as the guardian of national security demonstrates the recurrent and fundamental danger of the concept. Yet to argue against *any* role for the military, and more generally against the hitching of environmental issues to the notion of security, is to skirt a potentially fruitful site of conceptual and theoretical investigation. In any case, it is for the most part too late to avoid the connection. Deudney (1990) and Brock (1991) were no doubt right to caution against linkage. That the US security establishment has taken the concept on board, however, invalidates the questions why and why not in regard to environmental security. Instead, the question 'How can we contest and reclaim the concept of environmental security?' is the one that critical scholars should now be seeking to answer. The notion of environmental security and the policy implications that flow from it must now be contested at every turn.

8

Ecological Security
An Alternative Security Strategy

Much of the theory and practice of environmental security focuses on security aspects at the expense of environmental considerations. The environmental or ecological aspects are often emphasised through the concept of ecological security which, although somewhat undeveloped, implies a different security strategy from that of the prevailing approach.

Ecology and security

There is need for caution when referring to ecology in terms of security. Ecology is the study of the structure and functions of nature. Because most ecological theory is highly contested (Dovers *et al.* 1996: 1151), the use of the term in political theory and international relations generalises and possibly ignores important points of disagreement among ecologists themselves. Nevertheless, it can safely be said that 'ecological' security refers to a (normative) Green sentiment or outlook. This is ecology in the sense of a 'soft' and qualitative paradigm emphasising community, integrity and stability (Shrader-Frechette 1995: 126).

The concept of ecological security has evolved over the same period of time as environmental security. The distinction between the two is blurred as they are often used interchangeably, creating confusion for any discussion that seeks to distinguish one from the other. The principal difference is one of emphasis. Ecological security emphasises at least implicitly that it is ecosystems and ecological processes that should be secured; the *prima facie* referent is therefore non-human. Environmental security, for the most part, emphasises the state as the security referent, most often in a way that encourages military considerations to dominate, as is evident in the US response to and preoccupation with the environment–conflict thesis. Further, ecological security is used most often in reference to common security, whereas environmental security seems to be the preferred term of national security theory and policy. For example, the United Nations General Assembly has explored the possibility of an International Ecological Security System, UNEP has promoted the idea of ecological security, and Eduard Shevardnadze has talked of 'political ecology' in a speech to the UN in which he said that as 'a major component of international security, political ecology requires the involvement of the Security Council' (cited in Thomas 1992: 53).

As a means to distinguish ecological security from environmental security, Rogers defines ecological security as: 'the creation of a condition where the physical surroundings of a community provide for the needs of its inhabitants without diminishing its natural stock' (Rogers 1997: 30). This is not unlike the Ecological Economists' definition of sustainability (see Common and Perrings 1992, and Pezzey 1992). The distinction, for Rogers, is that environmental security refers more to the defence of natural resources, in effect a negative/reactive security like most prevailing conceptions of security, whereas ecological security refers to a positive security that seeks to maintain ecological equilibrium in the long term. The focus is thus on ecosystems as the referent object of security. The referent object is therefore reversed to make the biosphere the primary security referent. In this conceptualisation humans are secured only in so far as they inhabit the biosphere, and human activity is the principal threat to ecological security (a point lost on most environmental security analysts). Thus 'the danger arises not from what nature can do to the human, but rather the impact of human activities on nature and, in turn, the consequent effects on the human' (Mische 1989: 392).

Ecological security stems from a Green cosmology where systemic interdependence, complexity, uncertainty, harmony and sustainability are key themes. It calls for a shift in focus from individual and instrumental reason to a concern for the overall welfare of the planet. This challenges state-centred security theory and practice, and instead 'encourages, and in fact requires, that multiple actors become involved' (Rogers 1997: 30). It therefore offers a radical and more ecocentric approach to security, although the particulars of such an approach have yet to be articulated beyond the assertion that ecology helps to change mindsets, and from this all things good will result (Mische 1989). So, although it has emphasised the ecological dimension of ecological security, the literature has thus far said little about the specific security dimension. In this absence, the critical question is: why hitch ecology to security?

It is this question that most concerns Brock, who argues that the risk is that the concept – regardless of intent – 'may be invoked to defend the status quo of the present world ecological order, in which the distribution of benefits from environmental degradation is clearly in favour of the highly industrialized countries' (Brock 1992: 95). Brock is concerned that linking security with ecology may not result in the resolution of environmental and social problems. In this sense his question – 'Why not refer to sustainable development?' – is pertinent (Brock 1992: 94). The intent of ecological security, he answers, is to instrumentalise the high standing of security for environmental purposes (the tactic of securitisation). The pivotal issue in this debate is how security is understood. Mische, for example, conceives of security in terms of general threats to human and ecological well-being, as opposed to deliberate threats to the nation-state (Mische 1992). Thus there is a conflict of ontology and theory here that is reducible only by contestation of this 'power word' (Mische 1992: 105). This issue will be discussed further later in this chapter.

Ecological security may offer more than simply a raising of the profile of environmental problems. Soft ecological thought does indeed offer a different and non-instrumental world view, while hitching this to the concept of security potentially offers something that sustainable development does not do particularly well, which is incorporate issues of risk and resilience (remembering that security is at its core a discourse of risk). Thus for Mische:

> There is a need for some balance between risk and security, and the effort to arrive at some balance implies activity and change in response to changing conditions. Within living systems, including human social systems, security is not a fixed or steady state, but functions more like an organizing principle stimulating and steering a dynamic, evolutionary process. (Mische 1992: 105)

So resilience has potential as an organising principle for security, yet it has been largely unexplored in relation to ecological and environmental security. There is therefore a need to flesh out some dimensions of this ecology–resilience aspect.

Ecology, resilience and security

Ecological science is increasingly revealing that natural systems are complex, heterogeneous and subtle (Dovers *et al.* 1996). The principal lessons that have been drawn from ecology are: that all life depends on a complex web of food chains; that these chains involve plants and animals, energy, water, carbon, and nutrients; that there are thresholds below which the viability of a species may rapidly and perhaps irreversibly decline; and that simple ecosystems tend to be more unstable than complex ones (although this is contentious) (Pezzey 1992: 325). Another lesson from ecology is that there are finite limits imposed by energy and material availability, and hence there are limits to the growth of human systems (Meadows *et al.* 1972).

An important and often overlooked lesson from ecology is that ecological systems are constantly in short-term flux and long-term change. Dalby uses this as a metaphor for rethinking political change, arguing that it helps us to understand society as being in perpetual motion (Dalby 1998b). This dialectical perspective suggests that the realist tendency to resist change is irrational (unrealistic). The most crucial point about ecology, Dalby notes, is that the object of analysis is less the particular entity and more the complex and interconnected system in which it is situated. This can be seen in the increasing attention being given to ecological *processes* rather than single species or ecosystems in ecological research (and policy). Security from an ecological theory perspective therefore involves thinking about the whole rather than the parts. This means shifting the geographic focus from sharply delimited political spaces to a milieu of ill-defined locales in the broader setting of the earth. Politics therefore becomes less hierarchical and mechanical.

Ecological theory posits the notion of resilience to explain the character of ecological systems which are able to cope with major perturbations:

> Essentially, resilience in ecology is concerned with the longer-term survival and functioning of populations, species, and ecosystems in changing or fluctuating operating environments. Vulnerability, defined generally as susceptibility to injury, may be seen as inversely related to resilience: the more resilient, the less vulnerable. (Handmer and Dovers 1996: 486–7)

In ecological theory, resilience means the propensity of an ecosystem to retain its organisational structure following perturbation; in other words, the ability of a system to recover after sudden disturbances (Holling 1973). Ecosystem resilience is seen to be partly a function of the complexity of internal interactions between organisms. So, the more interconnectedness and complexity, the more resilient a system may be to perturbations. Generally speaking, individual species within an ecosystem are therefore more secure when the system is complex and diverse. As a metaphor for security, resilience suggests that human security is a function of social diversity and that security should be about reducing vulnerability to change (not resisting change *per se*). Accordingly, institutional plurality enhances social resilience (O'Riordan and Rayner 1991).

Resilience, and thus security, means fostering heterogeneity, keeping options open, and keeping a broad view (Handmer and Dovers 1996). These ideas are inherent in Bookchin's social ecology (Bookchin 1986). According to Bookchin, nature is a 'participatory realm of interactive life-forms whose most outstanding attributes are fecundity, creativity, and directiveness, marked by a complementarity that renders the natural world the grounding for an ethics of freedom rather than domination' (1986: 55). In this approach security is grounded in social diversity, the antithesis of realist theory which scripts all Others as dangerous, and so seeks social uniformity as a means to security. Further, just as diversity is a determinant of an ecosystem's resilience, social diversity, diversity of experience, and diversity of lifestyle provide the basis for a meaningful life, and a balance between humans and their habitat (ecological security).

This theme of diversity offers an interesting perspective on peace. Mische argues that 'respect for the diversity of life forms and a diversity of human cultures and expressions is vital to a Peace of the Earth' (1991: 142). Diversity also complements the poststructuralist concern for plurality where modernity is seen to stifle social, cultural and experiential diversity. Thus modernity is the antithesis and the downfall of security obtained through unity in diversity and complementary difference. Here we see, then, the starkest possible contrast between the prevailing conception of environmental security which seeks to secure modernity, and an ecological conception of security which seeks to overcome modernity and its homogenisation of life.

Ecological theory emphasises a cyclical conception of time as ecological processes are circular in nature: 'study biochemistry and you will see that all of nature's systems are circular designs. Nothing is linear, as most man made processes are' (Mathews 1993: 30). There is therefore a misfit between modern economic and political systems which are linear in nature, and natural processes. Prins interprets this to mean that there is a need to 'drive the linear logic of politics circular' (Prins 1990: 729). Further, ecological theory and the theory of evolution puts the temporal scale of human existence into perspective. If we remember that *Homo sapiens sapiens* has been in existence for approximately 100,000 of 4,000 million years of life on earth, it becomes apparent that humans are inconsequential in the scheme of evolution (although to be sure, humans have an unheralded capacity to destroy life). Even in this 100,000-year time-span it is only in the last 200 years that humans have had the capacity to alter natural systems seriously and irrevocably. The broad sweep of history thus demands humility and prudence with respect to human behaviour and the human claim to supremacy (among all species and among human cultures). This long-term perspective radically contextualises national political timeframes where all problems are held hostage to the two–four year electoral cycle (at least in liberal democracies).

There are also political-geographical implications of ecological theory. Because diverse and complex biophysical process are the sum of untold billions of minutiae, eventually totalling the entirety of the biosphere, the implication for human systems is the need for complex, interdependent, multi-level and cybernetic systems of governance. Eckersley, for example, recommends a multi-layered political structure which shifts authority both downward to local communities and upward to regional and global bodies, with authority allocated according to particular needs (Eckersley 1992). O'Riordan and Rayner also argue that to deal properly with the risk of global environmental change there needs to be a redistribution of power and 'self-reliant anarchic interconnectedness at both personal and communal levels' (1991: 97). Complete decentralisation lacks coordination, however, whereas complete governance from above means a lack of sensitivity to context: these issues are discussed further in Chapter 10. Nevertheless, an ecological view strongly suggests that the nation-state's dominance of formal politics and governance is inappropriate; it also problematises the theory and practice of sovereignty.

Ecology and sovereignty

Central to ecological theory (and the ecological outlook more generally) is the notion of interdependence. That ecological and human systems are fundamentally interdependent suggests that the drawing of political boundaries to delimit national sovereignty is extremely arbitrary; in Mische's terms, 'the Earth does not recognise sovereignty as we now know it' (Mische 1989: 394). Mische goes on to recommend a new philosophy of sovereignty which regards sovereignty as a:

> [D]ynamic, interactive process involving a system of relationships and a flow of energy and information between different spheres of sovereignty. Even among humans, sovereignty can dwell in more than one place at the same time: in a family, with parents, in people at local or national civic levels, in the state, in a global authority. (Mische 1989: 394)

This alternative geographical imagination challenges the exclusionary and simplistic view of the world as a series of homogeneous and independent political spaces defined by territorial boundaries. Despite this destabilisation of the ideal of sovereignty, however, the notion is not so amenable to manipulation. Westing (1989) and Byers (1991), who promote bioregions as the basis of a new political geography, also fail to grasp the full complexities of sovereignty. Because these proposals omit consideration of the *autonomy* that is integral to the theory and practice of sovereignty, they do not resolve the dilemmas of independence in an interdependent world (Stewart 1997). These proposals for a reconfiguration of sovereignty on ecological grounds make excessively general assumptions about sovereignty (Conca 1994a). Sovereignty entails a complex bundle of rights, some of which, such as non-intervention, are strongly asserted against certain claims that interdependence demands a revocation of sovereignty (Conca 1994a). This is certainly the case when wealthy countries exert pressure on pariah countries (which they construct). These are typically industrialising countries: for example, Brazil has 'earned' pariah status for its use of the Amazon forests. In response, these pariah countries (rightly) stress the sovereign right of non-intervention as a norm that must be preserved. It is thus a positive aspect of sovereignty that it is a means to resist globalisation from above, whether the pressure is applied through environmentally oriented discourses, such as that of the US, or the imposition of global economic regulation. In sum then, sovereignty is multi-faceted and complex, and this 'should make us humble about drawing general conclusions' (Conca 1994a: 708).

The most difficult aspect of new philosophies of sovereignty is that they tend to describe a geographical vision which, as they are post-sovereignty are also anti-autonomy and hence anti-rights. In undoing rights, they also elude the inseparable notion of responsibility. It is not so much that *sovereignty* resides in multiple places and contexts, it is that individuals and social groups (including states) have multiple rights and responsibilities which now interact at a scale that includes the global environs as well as the immediate locale. This is not to suggest that re-imagining politics is easy. It is the contention of this book, however, that what is required is not a reconfiguration of sovereignty as such, but rather a new vision of politics that emphasises responsibility.

When ecological problems become security problems

Some critics of ecological security argue that it degrades the analytical and normative significance of the concept of security (Deudney 1991, Stoett 1994, Levy 1995a). The prevailing national security agenda is far more robust than this, however, not least because of its ability to coopt and appropriate conceptual threats and turn these to its advantage. Most importantly, though, if security loses its analytical and normative significance, this would be a positive outcome for peace and the environment given that in the name of security millions have been killed and trillions of dollars wasted on socially and environmentally destructive military programmes. Because security as presently practised by states is violent and wasteful, any loss of normative significance is a loss for the 'hawks' and a boon for the 'doves'.

Other critics argue that an all-encompassing notion of ecological security strips the concept of its value as a conceptual device for inform-ing policy (Graeger 1996, Keller 1997). Gleditsch suggests that if the con-cept is to be useful it should only include forms of environmental degradation which have impacts similar to war (Gleditsch 1994: 135). Such arguments are not particularly sensitive to the enormity of the eco-logical security problematic. What is being referred to (at least by Mische and Rogers) is the destruction of habitat (the global environs), so the ambit of ecological security will inevitably be broad. In this sense ecolog-ical security is another discourse that says, fundamentally, that we shouldn't ruin the environment. Therefore, the criticism that ecological security is too ill-defined stems from an ignorance (be it active or passive) of the magnitude of environmental problems. Further, it might also be said that, rather than being imprecise, the concept of ecological security is indeed more precise than that of environmental security. Where the concept of environment can literally be interpreted to mean everything there is, the concept of ecology refers more specifically to natural systems.

Nevertheless the question 'When are environmental issues security issues?' has some validity, at least because there is a need to prioritise policy responses (Shaw 1996: 39). Put another way, some issues may be important enough to warrant 'securitising' as a means to prompt an extraordinary policy response. Certain criteria can be used to argue that particular ecological issues warrant consideration as matters of security.

There are three obvious parameters which help to frame identification of important ecological, hence security, problems; these are time, space and impact (Dovers 1995). Dovers et al. (1996) provide a broad three-tiered framework that serves as a filter for prioritising policy problems. They identify micro-, meso-, and macro- problems. *Micro*-problems are spatially and temporally discrete; they are generally local or sectoral; they are not particularly complex, nor is there much uncertainty; and their resolution is not necessarily expensive and can generally be achieved through existing policy mechanisms. An example of a micro-problem would be the need to manage or provide for the recovery of a single species or vegetation reserve. Micro-problems, then, clearly do not warrant extraordinary responses or a new conceptual or policy paradigm. *Meso*-problems are for the most part major issues but they are often contained within a country, and can be addressed fully by that country. An example of a meso-problem would be the conservation of a species across a broad geographical range. Meso-problems are thus significant, but do not pose systemic threats to patterns of consumption or production, nor do they require a fundamental reform of existing policy procedures. Meso-problems may be seen to be of relevance to national security, but in most instances do not warrant extraordinary responses nor new ways of conceiving of them. *Macro*-problems are 'multi-faceted, complex, fraught with uncertainties, spatially and temporally diffuse, highly connected to other issues, and threaten major disruption of human and natural systems' (Dovers et al. 1996: 1146). Examples of macro-problems include biodiversity loss and climate change. These are, in Dunn's (1981) terms, poorly structured policy problems, and they require a form of 'post-normal science' to take account of their complexity (Funtowicz and Ravetz 1991). Following this framework, ecological security issues are – at a minimum – these macro-problems.

Another rough filter comes from Handmer (1996a). From a risk perspective, Handmer proposes that the problems which warrant most attention (and hence are ecological security problems) are those which are largely invisible, unbounded, generally feared and a source of anxiety; that tend to contaminate rather than directly damage; that are generally irreversible and not self-recovering; and that are characterised by profound ignorance. This type of framework points to subtle and complex ecological damage. Toxic wastes and radiation contamination are the most obvious examples of these new species of problem (Erikson 1995). Such a framework implies that, in addition to natural hazards, there may be ecological emergencies such as the introduction of rapacious pathogens or the accidental release of toxic substances into ecosystems. The concept of ecological security would appear to have potential in this respect.

Perhaps the most comprehensive framework for scaling and framing ecological security problems comes from Dovers (1995). Dovers identifies six problem-framing attributes: the spatial scale of causes and effects, the magnitude of possible impacts, the temporal scale of possible impacts, the reversibility of impacts, the measurability of factors and processes, and the degree of complexity and connectivity. Those environmental problems which rate highly in each parameter should be considered as security issues, therefore warranting extraordinary policy responses. Three issues neatly fall into this framework: biodiversity loss, climate change and depletion of the ozone layer.

Biodiversity entails species diversity and genetic endowment; it is the very essence of evolution and species survival (Wilson 1992). Its loss is a loss which affects the survival chances of all species, including humans. The causes of biodiversity loss are well known: logging, clearing for agriculture, urban sprawl, exotic species, and extension of monocultures all reduce areas of genetic diversity. These same activities also cause habitat fragmentation, which reduces the resilience of these areas to climatic variation. Pollution and the extension of infrastructure also serve to lessen the integrity of biodiversity-rich areas. Following Dovers's framework, biodiversity loss qualifies as an ecological security issue because it is global in scope; its impacts concern survival in fundamental ways; the problem has evolved over a long period of time and is not easily – if at all – reversed; it is complex in scope; and is difficult for contemporary political and economic systems to accommodate. Biodiversity is an issue that gets little mention under the ambit of security because it is complex, resists simplistic linkages with conflict, and involves a degree of ecological sensitivity to which the prevailing security policy community is immune.

Climate change is similarly of such a scope that it warrants urgent attention and securitisation. Climate change is global in scope; its impacts are by most estimates likely to be very severe; it is a long-term and potentially 'runaway' issue which is not reversible except in the very long term (and such a reversal, if at all possible, will be by natural more than by human intervention); and its degree of connectivity is probably higher than that for any other contemporary issue. Climate change is complex and difficult for political and economic systems to deal with. In terms of policy responses, addressing climate change requires wide and deep structural reform of contemporary high-energy societies through a combination of less energy use, greater energy efficiencies and the application of non-polluting energy technologies. Additionally, the knowledge and technologies learned in the North should be freely available to the South. The problem of climate change thus strikes at the heart of the Western development model based on both increasing applications of energy and comparative advantage. The non-resolution of climate change is less a function of the failure of knowledge about the policies and methods necessary for reform, and more a function of the lack of political will to implement reforms. In this respect 'securitising' climate change to motivate action is justifiable.

Depletion of atmospheric ozone also registers as an environmental security issue in Dovers's framing and scaling analysis. The chlorofluorocarbons which break down ozone are emitted from millions of sources from individual aerosol cans to industrial plants; the impacts are similarly widespread, with increased ultraviolet radiation mainly (but not only) in lower latitudes. As well as being widespread in spatial scale, the impacts of ozone depletion are severe, with changes in ecosystem health as indicated by its suspected role in the decline of certain frog species, and increased rates of cancer in human populations in lower latitudes. Fortunately, despite its evolution over some time, the problem of ozone depletion is reasonably reversible. It does not register as a major problem on Dovers's response-framing criteria (Dovers 1995). In this respect ozone depletion is less of an environmental security problem than biodiversity loss or climate change.

Rather than determining ecological security problems in terms of their commensurability with warfare, Dovers's framework is a valid, more rigorous and more ecologically informed basis upon which to determine when certain problems merit consideration as security problems. A further issue, that of accidental releases from nuclear reactors, also arguably qualifies as an ecological security issue (see Barnett 1997).

Concepts and the contestation of security

Ecological security is a potentially valuable way of thinking about security, especially when it incorporates the notion of resilience. Applied to security, resilience means embracing diversity and complexity; this stands in contrast to existing practices of national security which deny and oppress these qualities. Nevertheless, the concept is perhaps more useful to ecologists than to the Green and peace movements.

In some respects the concept of ecological security shares the same difficulties that plague environmental security. It risks a militarisation of Green issues; it entrenches rather than undermines national power; and it invokes inappropriate responses. Conca argues that ecological security reinforces notions of stasis, militarises the environmental agenda, bolsters sovereignty, and mixes metaphors so that it becomes harder to define and act to bring about a peaceful and ecologically sustainable world (Conca 1994b: 18). The principal dilemma, he argues, is that 'the cost of elevating ecology to the level of a national-security concern may be its militarisation' (1994b: 19). Hence the 'securitisation' issue re-emerges. If ecological security is a Trojan horse that seeks to reform the meaning of security by working from within, then according to Conca, it has been captured and redeployed in conceptual counter-attacks.

Despite seeking to undermine prevailing practices of national security and sovereignty, proponents of ecological security have not had the same impact on the dominant discourse as counter-hegemonic proponents of environmental security such as (for example) Brown (1977) and Mathews (1989). One need look no further for proof of this than that 'ecological security' is never used by the US security establishment, nor by the vast majority of authors who write about environment–security linkages. This is a problem of the politics of discourse. To continue the analogy, this book contends that the Trojan horse of ecological security has been left outside the gates of the national security fortress, whereas environmental security has been wheeled inside. So, although ecological security speaks

to the whole issue of environment and security in important and innovative ways, it is, in effect, not heard by the mainstream. Ecological security
does not do what 'environmental security' does so well – that is, contest
the terminology and the discursive terrain of national security. It is this
contestation that in part makes environmental security valuable. In
deploying alternative language ecological security is marginal to this discursive contest.

To be sure, there is something to be said for using new words to
address old problems. As has been shown, environmental security is a
somewhat risky venture for proponents of a Green and peaceful future. In
this sense environmental security is a form of conceptual speculation
where the concept is ventured in order to gain (potentially) a renegotia-
tion of the conceptual bases of security. The danger is the colonisation of
the concept, as has occurred in the US. Using new words like ecological
security may temporarily avert this danger. The potential gain of this
speculative exercise, however, is the destabilisation of national security
discourse and practice by highlighting its contradictions and discontinu-
ities. Ultimately this may lead to its collapse, to a more benign synthesis,
or to the abandonment of the term by security policy makers and commentators. Although the negative outcome of securitising environmental
issues is real, the positive outcome is arguably worth striving for. This
contest is one in which ecological security has not played a key role
because of its alternative vocabulary. It may seem pedantic to deny the
efficacy of ecological security because of the word 'ecological' as opposed
to 'environmental', but in the realm of discourse key words matter.

This issue of contest and cooption is not new. The history of political
discourse is a history of deploying words as signs, symbols and metaphors
to legitimate a particular goal, be it the status quo or some other preordained outcome. This is the essence of counter-revolution (the continuous capture, emptying and subsequent redeployment of words and
ideas that initially threaten). This is the fate of *peace* when paired to war;
of *socialism* when used by apologists of cronyism; of *defence* when used to
justify attack; of *free speech, democracy, freedom, liberty* and *rights* as justifica-
tions for verbal abuse, the politics of hatred, the freedom to do violence,
the liberty to engage in labour exploitation, and the right to bear arms; it
is also the fate of sustainable development. The answer is not to abandon
the language of peace and hope, but to defend it. Abandoning a term
because it is corrupted is to retreat from the struggle for a better future.

Throwing up new terms to be appropriated does not stop the problem. This is the unwitting deeper failing of ecological security; it is a sympathetic bystander on the sidelines of the substantive contest.

To conclude, although ecological security has many strengths, it fails to engage effectively in a fundamental function of environmental security – the contestation and delegitimisation of security itself. For this reason this book prefers to maintain the label 'environmental security', but to empty it of its existing meaning and refill it with notions of human security and positive peace (the function of the following chapter). Putting people first in this way does not mean ignoring the lessons of ecology. The principal difference is that putting people first and retaining the label maintains the ability to contest the substantive issue of what security is and for whom it applies. So, many of the themes and ideas discussed in this chapter are of relevance to the next chapter's reformulation of environmental security, and these should be borne in mind throughout the remainder of this book.

9

Environmental Security for People

The meaning of environmental security must be reconsidered if the concept is to make any meaningful contribution to the environment or human security. The principal failings of environmental security as presently conceived can be summarised as follows: it propagates the environmentally degrading security establishment; it talks in terms of, and prepares for, war; it defends the environmentally destructive modern way of life; and it ignores the needs and desires of most of the world's population. In short, at present, environmental security secures the processes that destroy the environment and create insecurity for the many for the benefit of the few. Ecological security has few such limitations, but fails to contest the meaning and practice of security because of the uncommon label 'ecological'.

What is required, then, is a reformulation of environmental security which does not prioritise national security and the issue of conflict above the needs of those who are most environmentally insecure. The approach that this book favours is to reformulate environmental security in terms of *human* security and peace, and drawing on the insights of ecological security. Taking the concept of security away from the state and towards people in this way 'points to a serious political project' (Walker 1987: 25). In this vein, the remainder of this book seeks to make some preliminary inroads into a new politics for a reformulated, human–centred concept of environmental security.

Reclaiming security

As a general rule, security is a function of power. The more power a person or group has to shape social life to suit their ends, the more secure they will tend to be. Those with less power tend to be more insecure: the landlord tends to be more economically secure than the tenant; the General is more secure from warfare than the foot soldier; and the food producer enjoys greater food security than the dependent food purchaser. Insecurity is therefore relative, and is a product of a broad milieu of social exchanges. This understanding of security and power is supported by Booth, for whom security defined as 'power over' occurs at the expense of others: 'true (stable) security can only be achieved by people and groups if they do not deprive others of it' (Booth 1991: 319). This suggests that any new approach to security must be based on the principles of equity and justice if it is to be sustained. In this respect socialism (however unfashionable it may now be in academic circles) is relevant to security.

From the advent of European colonisation through to contemporary globalisation, the concentration and centralisation of power has grown, and with it the geographic spread and degree of insecurity. Indeed, however nebulous, the phenomenon of globalisation (or at least enhanced economic integration) has heightened insecurity for the vast majority of people who are increasingly unable to control the economic environment which determines the provision of their most basic needs. This same economic system is also responsible for the degradation of the physical environment from which basic subsistence needs could formerly have been extracted with relative certainty. Certain insecurities are reasonably common, perhaps the first of these being the prospect of exposure to nuclear weapons. Yet many widespread insecurities, such as economic insecurity, are by no means universally experienced.

What is notable about this late-modern era is the relative impotence of the state to control the terms of security. The state is increasingly unable to act as regulator between global dynamics (such as speculative capital moving instantly through dense communication networks, or the illegal movement of drugs, weapons and people through the proliferation of cheap and rapid transport), and local places. In this respect initiatives to uniformly (de)regulate trade and investment, such as the WTO, can be read as proof that sovereignty no longer provides comprehensive security. Further, even the traditional concern for national security from external aggression is harder to control given the proliferation of weapons of mass destruction and the sophisticated nature of terrorism.

Security is the litmus test of sovereignty, and sovereignty is a cornerstone of modern politics. That there is less security for most people in most places suggests that this foundation of modern politics is being battered by globalisation. Another cornerstone is the common identity shared by all which is embodied in 'the nation', a construction whose necessary particularity is increasingly difficult to sustain in a world of cultural interpenetration facilitated by cheaper, faster and proliferating communication (and transport) technologies. While this may be construed as a crisis, the positive potential is that a different conception of politics and community might emerge (and some would say is emerging), which gives priority to difference, pluralism, conversation, and openness (Walker 1987).

This alternative politics is evident in critical social movements. The lesson learned from these movements is that insecurity takes many forms, and so approaches to security must be diverse, multi-dimensional, and located at many levels of society (Walker 1988). A single dominant security concept (such as national security) therefore does not satisfy the full range of security needs of people. Rethinking security therefore involves rethinking the relationship between security and political practice. A necessary first step is the democratisation of security issues: 'security is not something that can be left to someone else ... effective security must mean democratic security' (Walker 1988: 126). To this end the work of non-governmental organisations assists in building an alternative, action-based politics based on interconnected, globally aware communities (Boulding 1988).

Human security

In this context of late-modern politics, security has been liberated somewhat from the clutches of the state, so that now its meaning and practice can be contested more openly. This explains the genesis of environmental security, a sectoral categorisation (identifying a risk domain) which does not necessarily identify a referent to be secured (who is at risk). Another, not incompatible way of contesting and extending the concept of security involves prioritising the needs of people above the needs of the nation-state. Thus the notion of human security has been proposed. Human security says little about sectors (it does not explicitly classify sources of risk), but much about the referent to be secured (people). Human-centred conceptions of security begin by asking the question: *whose security?* This is a subversive question which casts into doubt the state's monopolisation of political legitimacy and violence (Walker 1987). Asking it opens up space to consider alternative meanings and referents of security, as well as alternative strategies.

The United Nations Development Programme (UNDP) uses the concept of human security to assist in the framing of development and justice issues. The UNDP adopts a comprehensive approach to human security, identifying seven sectors or domains: economic, food, health, environmental, personal, community, and political (1994). The 1994 *Human Development Report* says that:

> Human security is people-centred. It is concerned with how people live and breathe in a society, how freely they exercise their many choices, how much access they have to market and social opportunities – and whether they live in conflict or peace. (p. 23)

> In the final analysis, human security is a child who did not die, a disease that did not spread, a job that was not cut, an ethnic tension that did not explode in violence, a dissident who was not silenced. Human security is not a concern with weapons – it is a concern with human life and dignity. (p. 22)

The contribution of UNDP enhances the legitimacy of efforts to contest and reclaim the meaning and practice of security.

Human security requires the provision of basic material needs such as nutritious food, clean air and water, and shelter (as identified by the UNDP). There is a range of additional requirements, however, that are fundamental to an individual's existential well-being and security: an emotional support network for giving and receiving care; strong family ties; opportunities for extended community interaction; a diverse and stimulating environment; opportunities for creative expression and learning; opportunities for spontaneous behaviour; and a personal sense of involvement, purpose, belonging, excitement, challenge, satisfaction, love, enjoyment and confidence (Boyden 1987: 79). This view is explicitly linked to security by Tickner, who argues that the desire for close relationships and belonging are undervalued aspects of human nature, and should form the basis of a more humane approach to security (Tickner 1992).

Human security, as seen by this book at least, accepts Gandhi's radically challenging hypothesis (1951) that historically non-violence has been the normal state of affairs between humans. On this basis, then, the traditional practice of basing security strategy on the assumption that violence is the default condition does injustice to the processes which historically have ensured survival (Clements 1990). Thus good faith and trust become genuine factors in decision-making about human security. Because (most) people learn basic lessons about trust and security in close personal relationships, the principles that underlie these can be used to inform relationships between social groups, including states. Thus because the micro can influence the macro, the personal is inherently political, and 'issues of global security are interconnected with, and partly constituted by, local issues; therefore the achievement of comprehensive security depends on action by women and men at all levels of society' (Tickner 1992: 142).

Alternative approaches to security are 'dissident discourses' (Dalby 1996b). They are engaged in a conception of politics that transcends the state, understanding security not so much in the negative sense of protecting the status quo, but as the positive task of establishing and then maintaining basic human rights, justice and freedom. They are engaged in a contestation and reclamation of the concept of security to serve people and positive peace. These radical approaches are attuned to what Walker calls the 'dialectical interplay between security and insecurity' in human affairs, where vulnerability is not necessarily a negative phenomenon, but rather: 'to be vulnerable is to be open. To be open is to create the opportunity for communication and exchange, for learning and commitment' (Walker 1988: 126, 127). Security therefore entails balancing risks and fears with trust and dialogue.

At the 1997 people's Conference on Alternative Security Systems in the Asia–Pacific a declaration was passed which points to the future of a critically aware theory and practice of security. The Declaration was produced by concerned people in the industrialising world, and thus is more reflective of the concerns and needs of the most vulnerable of people. It stated that:

> Security must be fundamentally redefined, democratised and reclaimed by people. It must replace narrow state, military or market interests with comprehensive human security which includes the social, cultural, gender, economic and environmental aspects of security. It must also recognise the need for peace-building and the prevention of violent conflict. This requires both a transformation of existing structures and relationships and the creation of new structures and relationships which include groups previously marginalised.
>
> Real security is based on establishing democratic relations among men and

women, within societies, between people and the state and between states themselves, and within international institutions. Establishing substantive democracy is fundamental.

(*Democratising Security: Declaration of the Conference on Alternative Security Systems in the Asia Pacific*, 1997, http://www.nautilus.org).

Thinking in terms of human security shifts the scale of analysis away from nations to the local level. It focuses on the immediate vulnerability of most of the world's population, as opposed to hypothetical threats to nation-states. It provides a referent object which, when combined with environmental concerns, forms the basis for a new approach to environmental security.

Environmental security as human security

A human-centred environmental security concept places the welfare of people first and prioritises the welfare of the most disadvantaged above all else. This is consistent with the discussion of environmental insecurity presented in Chapter 2. A human-centred approach is justified on moral grounds and, in a more pragmatic way, because addressing the welfare of the most disadvantaged means addressing many of the future sources of environmental degradation; as Sachs says, 'protecting the rights of the most vulnerable members of our society ... is perhaps the best way we have of protecting the right of future generations to inherit a planet that is still worth inhabiting' (Sachs 1996: 151). This should not obscure the responsibility for poverty and environmental degradation that rests primarily with the well-off in industrialised countries.

This human-centred environmental security concept sees the enhancement of welfare, peace and justice as the fundamental purpose of politics. Peace and justice are the firmest pillars on which to build exactly the sort of authoritative yet genuinely legitimate institutions required for human and environmental security (Conca 1994c). Linking environmental security to peace in this way is supported by the recent linkage of environmental problems with human rights. For example, in 1990 the UN General Assembly agreed that 'all individuals are entitled to live in an environment adequate for their health and well-being'; and in 1995 the UN Commission on Human Rights passed a resolution that 'environmental damage has potentially negative effects on human rights and the enjoyment of life, health, and a satisfactory standard of living' (both cited in Cherry 1996: 3). As argued for here, environmental security is very much about the rights of all people to a healthy environment. Further, in so far as rights are meaningless without responsibilities, environmental security means all people have a responsibility to behave in such a way as to not impinge on the rights of others to a healthy environment.

This approach to environmental security argues that the primary purpose of the nation-state is to meet the basic needs of all people. This means that the interests of the state should be subordinate to the interests of people, and, as theoretically justified, that the state is not apart from, but is of the people. Thus environmental insecurity is seen not as a problem for the legitimacy and survival of modern institutions, but as a problem for which modern institutions are responsible. Those institutions that are most problematic, such as the military, are those that must be reformed first. This does not mean a naive hope that the military will see the error of its ways and atone; it means thinking seriously and acting carefully to achieve gradual and progressive reform.

This human-centred conceptualisation of environmental security does not concern itself with the possibility that environmental degradation may induce violent conflict. This is not seen as the most pressing problem: environmentally induced warfare is much less likely than most would suggest; is even less likely in a world where all people are environmentally secure; and the threat of it is often used to justify practices which are counterproductive to environmental balance and human security (see Chapter 5). Removing the warfare aspect from environmental security removes the basis upon which strategic rationality gains entry into the concept. Because rethinking security means rethinking politics, the continued saturation of contemporary politics with issues and metaphors of violence needs to be avoided.

In contrast to thinking about violent conflict, a human-centred conceptualisation of environmental security asserts the need for cooperation and inclusion to manage the environment for the equal benefit of all people and future generations. Support for this approach to environmental management is a key message of the 1992 Earth Summit (UNCED 1993). In Australia, cooperation, inclusion and conflict resolution are central to successful resource management institutions. This is demonstrated by high rates of community participation in Landcare and Total Catchment Management (Campbell 1994); it is proven in the effectiveness of intergovernmental institutional arrangements such as the

Great Barrier Reef Marine Park Authority and the Murray Darling Basin Commission; and it underlies the success of informal non-government agreements such as the Cape York cooperative management agreement between Aboriginal, industrial and Green groups. In the South Pacific, despite enormous environmental pressures, regional agreements and institutions such as the South Pacific Regional Environment Programme (SPREP) are successfully addressing environmental problems in cooperative and peaceful ways. Inclusion, mediation and cooperation are therefore key themes for environmental security.

Defining environmental security

All definitions are problematic (Tennberg 1995); in this book, nevertheless, environmental security is defined as 'the process of peacefully reducing human vulnerability to human-induced environmental degradation by addressing the root causes of environmental degradation and human insecurity'. Put another, more axiomatic way, environmental security is the process of minimising environmental insecurity.

There is a danger that this definition dichotomises humans and nature, a problem that also vexes ecological security. It is important to be clear, then, about the deeper implication of this definition. Humans are seen as nature rendered self-conscious (Bookchin 1982). This means, in Saurin's words, that humans are not counterposed to nature, but are 'constitutive of nature' (1996: 83). Accordingly, the definition's reference to 'human-induced environmental degradation' means not the degradation of an external or Other habitat, but of the habitat of humans themselves. Environmental degradation can thus be read as human degradation. In this way this book is not opposed to definitions of environmental (or ecological) security which seek to make the biosphere the referent of security, because securing the biosphere means securing the physical bases of human health and well-being. Nevertheless, the principal referent here is humans, as this is arguably a keener political incentive – which is to say that a concern for the environment *per se* is less likely to mobilise action (the problem with Deep Green ecophilosophy).

This definition seeks to treat the underlying *causes* that create environmental degradation. Environmental security as an absolute condition is arguably impossible, not least because security is a highly relative concept. Instead, like peace and sustainability, environmental security should be seen as a systemic goal. Defining environmental security as a process in this way overcomes the hitherto strong equation of security with stasis. Security as a process means ongoing monitoring and adaptation of programmes and policies. In this way security becomes an adaptive process which is sensitive to change and seeks to manage change peacefully (rather than defend against it).

The relationship between national security and human security warrants brief consideration. National security and human security are not necessarily mutually exclusive. At present, however, the issues of concern to (and the strategies to procure) national security are counterproductive to human security within and beyond any given nation-state. Although in theory the nation-state is obliged to provide human security, the continuing emphasis on conflict, threats and (scripted) malignant Others makes genuine security elusive. Environmental security demands that nation-states act domestically and in concert to curb global, regional and local processes that generate environmental degradation and human insecurity. This will necessitate stronger government on some issues, and conceding authority in others.

It was argued earlier that to be useful any approach to security must be able to answer a number of basic questions. In response to the question *whose security?* environmental security seeks the security of the individual and local groups, and more immediately the security of those people who are most vulnerable to the effects of environmental degradation. In response to the question *security from what?* environmental security addresses the impacts of environmental degradation on humans, including lack of clean water, malnutrition, inadequate access to energy for cooking and heating (most acute in the problem of fuelwood shortages), high infant mortality rates and maternal death rates, exposure to preventable debilitating or fatal illnesses, and greater exposure and vulnerability to risks such as floods, fires, earthquakes, tsunamis, cyclones, droughts and famines. This then leads to the question *insecurity how?* – the answer to which is the impoverishment of people and the degradation of nature largely through political-economic processes. Thus the problem is not humankind's struggle with nature, but humankind's struggle with the dynamics of its own cultures (de Wilde 1996).

This human-centred conceptualisation of environmental security is informed in part by ecology and hazards theory. These offer a new basis for thinking about security and politics, and central to this are the notions of risk, vulnerability and resilience.

Risk

Risk is a subjectively interpreted and therefore highly political phenomenon. For example, in the prevailing approach to national security those who identify the risks identify only those possibilities which may jeopardise their particular vested interests. Hence environmental security in US security policy discourse is concerned with those particular risks to the interests of the US policy community, and not the risks that others in distant places experience. Rayner (1992) analyses risk from a cultural theory perspective and finds that – like the response of the US to environmental security – 'of all the things people can be worried about, they will be inclined to select for particular attention those risks that help to reinforce the social solidarity of their institutions' (Rayner 1992: 91). Hewitt also talks of the prevailing approach to risk (from a hazards perspective) in a way that might well refer to the dominant approach to environmental security:

> its strength depends less upon its logic and internal sophistications than on its being a convenient productive 'world view' for certain dominant institutions and academic spokesmen. In other words it is, above all, a construct reflecting the shaping hand of a contemporary social order. (Hewitt 1983: 4)

There is therefore more than one discourse of risk, and it seems that common to all are exclusions and inclusions, emphases and biases which serve the interests of the already powerful. Talking about risks therefore requires democratically 'negotiating' risk (Handmer 1996a).

This raises the need for some reflection on the reasons why this book finds particular risks and effects of environmental degradation to be problematic. In a general sense what this book does is reassert the moral imperative of meeting the needs of those people who have not benefited from modernity. It is possible to construct a rough typology of needs: there are basic health needs, basic social needs, equal opportunity needs, and relative consumption needs. Basic health needs are such things as clean water, sufficient nutritious food and access to a level of health and hygiene. These enable people to be free from unnecessary debilitating sickness. They also make death a less likely prospect at any stage of a person's life (and more a factor of old age or remote chance) as is the case for most people in the industrialised world. That one fifth of the world's people do not have their basic health needs satisfied is the fundamental injustice with which this book is concerned. That these people are also extremely vulnerable to perturbations in weather or economics is also of great concern: these are risks proper.

Basic social needs are the requirements of a meaningful existence. They include diversity of experience, close family and personal relationships, and a sense of responsibility (Boyden 1987). Many of these have been denied by modern ways of living. Equal opportunity needs are those requirements necessary for an individual to participate as an equal member in her particular society: for example, in many industrialised societies having access to an automobile is necessary for an individual to gain employment and meet the demands of urban life. Relative consumption needs, then, are needs that in their absence will not result in unnecessary illness or death, nor unequal opportunity. This relates to the consumption of luxury items.

The risks of concern to environmental security are those which are immediate and necessary to health and well-being (basic health needs). There are exclusions in this approach, namely that the needs of the wealthy come last. But inverting the priorities of the industrialised world and countering the culture of consumption in this way is morally defensible, and is a useful strategy to reveal the contradictions of modernity and to begin to address a better future for all people.

Effective risk management requires a holistic approach which connects technical and political strategies, and which involves all people in ways that are cumulatively preventive. Decisions as to how to manage risk cannot be based solely on technical criteria or expert judgements; participatory decision-making procedures capable of accounting for moral and lifestyle choices are necessary (O'Riordan and Rayner 1991: 98). This points to social processes, empowerment and democracy as means to lessen vulnerability, and to strategies for preventing risk-generating activity (for example, the use of solar power to avoid burning fossil fuels which contribute to climatic instability). Environmental security is about risk, and risk needs to be democratically negotiated to determine the most urgent risks and the best ways of dealing with them.

Vulnerability

Vulnerability is a defining characteristic of insecurity. It is a product of poverty, exclusion, marginalisation and inequities in material consumption. People's vulnerability, then, is generated by social, economic and political processes. The cyclone that struck the coastal region of Bangladesh in April 1991 demonstrated clearly the interdependence between environmental degradation, insecurity and vulnerability to hazards. Bangladesh is a low-lying country and has in excess of 100 million people with a high population density. Given that the country is one of the world's poorest, this population density creates pressures which force the poorest people to live and work in the marginal and shifting coastal zone. This in turn places pressure on coastal ecosystems which are denuded of stabilising vegetation, and this magnifies the vulnerability of these people to environmental perturbations. The April 1991 cyclone battered the coastal zone for nine hours and with it came a storm surge that raised water levels along the coast by up to seven metres. The death toll reached 139,000 and up to three million people were exposed to severe health risks; 118,000 acres of crops were damaged; 190,000 homes, 9,300 schools and over 3,000 freshwater wells were destroyed (AODRO 1991). A lack of physical and service infrastructure meant that many died from diseases and malnutrition after the event. The victims of this cyclone were already extremely insecure by any standard. Their vulnerability was fundamentally a function of poverty. The painful lesson (learned repeatedly elsewhere), is that enhancing security means eliminating poverty, and vice versa.

Resilience

Resilience is the inverse of vulnerability, and is hence reasonably synonymous with security. It entails being less susceptible to damage from both short-term changes (such as cyclones and currency fluctuations) and long-term changes (such as rising sea levels and declining terms of trade). It also refers to the capacity to recover from short-term changes and adapt to long-term changes.

Resilience is a function of power, diversity and interdependence. The question of empowerment, fundamental to contemporary political theory and practice, is addressed in the following chapter. Diversity is desirable because it facilitates flexibility and choice. For example, after a cyclone a community with a wide range of food plants will be more likely to have some food reserves intact than a community relying solely on bananas, and a woman with a diversity of skills is more likely than her colleagues to find new employment in the event of retrenchment. Interdependence among diverse entities enhances resilience, at least in the social realm, as networks of reciprocity enable sharing of one group's burden among many related groups (which at the international scale is the essence of emergency relief). Enhancing resilience therefore involves making full use of diverse social resources such as cooperatives, churches and self-help groups. Resilience is about the ability of a group to draw on material and social resources for recovery from shocks, making traditional coping strategies just as relevant as institutional and technological strategies (Handmer 1996b).

Flexibility is also achieved through designing some 'slackness' into human systems (Handmer and Dovers 1996). Maintaining spare financial and material resources in social and ecological systems enables a surplus to be drawn on in times of difficulty. For example, a budget surplus hedges against welfare restrictions in times of economic downturn; vacant high land can be used as a safety zone in response to tsunami; food and water reserves kept aside ease recovery and minimise losses after cyclones; household savings ease the burden in the event of unemployment; and a healthy and well-nourished body is more likely to survive a season of drought than one already malnourished. In research conducted in West Africa, Mortimore (1989) found that resilience to drought was a function of flexibility in the use of labour, crop location in space and time, choice of crops to grow, and means of earning income. Flexible strategies demand vision and restraint from the dictum of optimum and maximal use of resources (Handmer and Dovers 1996).

Short-term strategies such as those discussed above are all important in enhancing the resilience of people to the day-to-day effects of environmental degradation as well as to disasters, but the long-term reduction of risk, vulnerability and insecurity requires fundamental changes in the institutions and beliefs of modernity. There will be no lasting environmental security unless these changes take place. Changes in power relations – a minimum requirement – can be achieved by extending democracy, enhancing political participation and improving governance. These issues are explored in the following chapter.

Environmental security and sustainability

The main concepts presently being used to address environmental problems are sustainable development and sustainability. Sustainable development involves a humanitarian element not unlike the value this book discovers in environmental security. It recognises that the problem lies in the disparities among people as well as the degradation of eco-systems (WCED 1987, UNCED 1993). The principal dilemma with sustainable development is the word 'development', which implies that development *per se* is not the problem; rather, it is the particular environmental effects of existing development practices that need to be addressed (see Redclift 1987, Sachs 1993). Of course, this depends on what one means by 'development', in the same way that the meaning of environmental security is contingent on the meaning of 'security'.

The concept of sustainability has evolved from sustainable development, and is now the preferred term of many because it avoids (at least semantically) the difficulty with the word development. Dovers defines sustainability as 'the ability of a natural, human, or mixed system to withstand or adapt to, over an indefinite time scale, endogenous or exogenous changes perceived as threatening' (Dovers 1997: 304). The difference between sustainable development and sustainability, then, is that sustainability is the system property and goal, whereas sustainable development is the policy activity aimed at achieving that goal (Dovers 1997: 304). Sustainability is concerned with a number of issues, including the structure of the economy, discounting (of the future), depletion of natural resources and environmental degradation, population growth, and sectoral sustainability (Pezzey 1992). Exploitation and equity are, by Pezzey's reckoning at least, secondary concerns. Sustainability is still therefore largely an economic paradigm, albeit one which is highly critical of conventional neo-classical economics (Common 1995). The meaning of sustainability is also somewhat ambiguous, yet paradoxically this enhances its popularity in that ambiguity makes it safe to use. Sustainable development, sustainability, and environmental security are thus all plagued by an ambiguity which makes them amenable to appropriation by vested interests. This is the nature of concepts: they are contested, but such contests are one of the ways in which society negotiates its values and goals.

This book's reformulated concept of environmental security differs from, but complements, sustainability for a number of reasons. First, like sustainable development, issues of exploitation and equity are primary rather than secondary concerns. In this sense environmental security is compatible with the concept of environmental justice, which focuses on the discrimination inherent in the exposure of certain groups to environmental hazards. Second, environmental security explores the juncture of security/foreign policy and the environment. This is an area less explicitly covered in sustainability and sustainable development, and it is this (original) explicit international focus that is one of environmental security's distinguishing characteristics. In this respect environmental security serves a useful function in that it facilitates communication between a diverse range of interests (Brock 1997). Third, environmental security is concerned with the environmental impacts of military activities and explores the possibility of greening the military. Fourth, environmental security adds to the Rio Declaration's assertion that peace and environmental protection are interdependent and indivisible (UNCED 1993). It does this by understanding environmental degradation to be the product of violence both direct and structural.

Perhaps the most important contribution of environmental security is its political dimension. Whereas sustainable development and sustainability are still largely concerned with economics (of development and *ecological* economics respectively), environmental security is fundamentally concerned with politics. The issue is not just one of the politics of security as addressed in most of this book, but also one of what a reformulated notion of security holds for politics itself.

Concepts and the contestation of security revisited

A final and notable distinction of environmental security as opposed to sustainability is that environmental security seeks to securitise environmental problems, thereby making them more important than other politicised issues. Environmental security as presented here agrees that environmental degradation is a security issue, but security is seen as human security. If there is any truth in the original declared function of the state as provider of security to its citizens, then the state – so the argument runs – must respond to environmental insecurity with the same unrestrained vigour that it adopts to ensure military security. Environmental (human) security takes this security justification of the state seriously. It assumes that the primary purpose of government is to ensure that the basic needs of people are satisfied. This is the political intent of environmental security; it stems from the intuitive resonance and appeal of security, and it contests the meaning and practice of security because it is the favoured term of political discourse in this late modern era.

The question of whether it is valid to understand environmental problems as security problems recurs throughout any thoughtful discussion of environmental security. The dilemma should by now be apparent; securitising environmental issues runs the risk that the strategic/realist approach will coopt and colonise the environmental agenda rather than respond positively to environmental problems (as discussed in Chapter 6). For this reason critics of environmental security, such as Deudney (1991) and Brock (1991), suggest that it is dangerous to understand environmental problems as security issues. This book's position on the matter has been emerging in previous chapters. It contends that the problem turns not on the presentation of environmental problems as security issues, but on the meaning and practice of security in present times. Environmental security, wittingly or not, contests the legitimacy of the realist conception of security by pointing to the contradictions of security as the defence of territory and resistance to change. It seeks to work from within the prevailing conception of security, but to be successful it must do so with a strong sense of purpose and a solid theoretical base.

Understanding environmental problems as security problems is thus a form of conceptual speculation. It is one manifestation of the pressure the Green movement has exerted on states since the late 1960s. This pressure has pushed state legitimacy nearer to collapse, for if the state cannot control a problem as elemental as environmental degradation, then what is its purpose? This legitimacy problem suggests that environmental degradation cannot further intensify without fundamental change or the collapse of the state. This in turn implies that state-sanctioned environmentally degrading practices such as those undertaken in the name of national security cannot extend their power further if it means further exacerbation of environmental insecurity. While the system may resist environmental security's challenge for change, it must also resist changes for the worse. In terms of the conceptual venture, therefore, appropriation by the security apparatus of the concept of environmental security is unlikely to result in an increase in environmental insecurity (although the concept itself may continue to be corrupted). On the other hand, succeeding in the conceptual venture may mean a positive modification of the theory and practice of national security. It may also mean that national governments will take environmental problems more seriously, reduce defence budgets, and generally implement policies for a more peaceful and environmentally secure world. This dual goal of demilitarisation and upgrading policy may well be a case of wanting to have one's cake and eat it – but either the having or the eating is sufficient justification for the concept (Brock 1996).

The worst outcome would be if the state ceased to use the concept of environmental security, heralding the end of the contest and requiring that the interests of peace and the environment be advocated through alternative discourses. This is perhaps the only real failure that is likely to ensue from the project of environmental security.

The whole question of securitisation hinges, of course, on the meaning of security. The security component of environmental security as understood here is human-centred as opposed to nation-centred. Indeed, it directly contests the legitimacy of national security by challenging notions of threats and risks, and by questioning who is at risk. In this sense environmental security is as much about contesting a defining feature of modernity (national security) as it is about posing a new concept for dealing with environmental problems. Yet although this contest is a crucial function of environmental security, this book's reformulation of the concept also seeks to serve as a genuine alternative to understanding and addressing environmental problems.

A human-centred (as opposed to state-centred) concept of environmental security is consistent with the general direction of critical approaches to security. The consistency arises from the shared understanding that security is intuitively about the stable provision of basic needs – needs which states and the system of states have hitherto failed to provide. A strong, human-centred concept of environmental security can better contest the meaning of security in a way that, despite the concerns of critics, stands to gain much by highlighting the inherent contradictions of national security, yet stands to lose little from a failure to succeed in this venture. It may also serve as a valuable alternative concept to sustainable development and sustainability by highlighting the political aspects of environmental problems and their solutions, and by re-emphasising that environmental problems are very much problems of human vulnerability.

10

Towards Environmental Security

The implications of the concept of environmental security proposed in the previous chapter are broad. This is inevitably the case with any concept designed to frame, assess and resolve environmental problems, because environmental degradation is fundamentally a product of modernity. Thus wide-ranging and deep reform of social systems is required. The exact programme of action to pursue is by no means clear, although there are suites of well-established policy measures in existence. Nevertheless, in so far as (formal) politics is an activity where economic, social and cultural processes are theoretically, occasionally and potentially regulated to protect the greater good, it is appropriate to focus on political reform as a major task necessary to achieving environmental security.

This chapter seeks to explore possibilities for enhancing environmental security (and therefore human security and peace) through a 'revitalized' politics that enables better governance and policy (Rees 1994: 171). It speaks of these contentious and debated terms (policy, politics and governance) in particular ways. For the sake of clarity, then, policy is understood as a purposive course of action by an actor or actors to deal with problems (Anderson 1984). Governance is understood to be the mechanisms through which people and groups express their concerns, negotiate their differences, exercise their obligations and ensure fulfilment of their rights. Governance, then, refers to the way society steers itself (Rosenau 1995). Politics is understood in the Aristotelian tradition as the business of deliberation, negotiation and pursuit of the good, and in Crick's terms as 'that solution to the problem of order which chooses conciliation rather than violence and coercion' (Crick 1993: 30). Good governance is necessary for effective politics, but good governance is impossible in the absence of effective politics. Policy is the implementation of the good. The overall vision of this book is a revitalised politics and a system of governance which is 'polycentric' and multi-level (Pelling 1998: 1).

Limitations in the nature and structure of politics are increasingly seen as the biggest impediments to effective environmental policy. A number of United Nations conferences on the environment have proposed a range of policies which, if implemented, would enhance environmental security. Regardless of their limitations, the recommendations of the United Nations Conference on Environment and Development (UNCED 1993), if implemented in conjunction with those of the International Conference on Population and Development (ICPD 1994) and the Habitat II conference (UNCHS 1996), would provide a much higher degree of environmental security for the majority of the world's population. Comprehensive support for this view – that the problem is not the policies, but the politics – comes from the Earth Summit Plus Five special session of the United Nations. In reviewing the implementation of Agenda 21, this session noted the failure of the international system to act in the interests of sustainability (United Nations 1997). Addressing the session, the Executive Director of Greenpeace was blunt on this matter of political failure:

> [Y]ou [national governments] have failed as yet to act. You have given in to commercial interests; you have put national interests above the welfare of future generations … it has become fashionable to say that governments can do very little, and that all power now lies with unaccountable multinational companies and institutions in a newly globalised market. But let that not disguise the power and accountability which you, together, hold to impose environmental and social limits, controls and standards. (Bode 1997: 1–3)

Environmental problems need political solutions. The failure to act is therefore fundamentally a failure of politics and governance, and it is these failures that this book now tentatively begins to address.

Two broad principles underpin this chapter's vision of revitalised politics and polycentric governance. First, individual action can alter the structures of power. This is based on the premise that while structures influence agency, agency can influence structures (Giddens 1984). Second, politics and democracy can be revitalised through enhanced communication, dialogue, or conversation between parties (Dryzek 1990). Both principles are well established in contemporary social theory, but are nevertheless problematic. This does not mean that they should be abandoned; they are, in this book's view, persuasive.

The following discussion should not be read as one author's blueprint for a new world order. These are suggestions made to demonstrate the possibilities of a revitalised and more personal politics and a more responsive system of governance. Dryzek provides a timely warning here:

> If the twentieth century holds one political lesson, it is that we should beware of anyone peddling ... blueprints, be they socialist paradises, fascist Reichs to last a thousand years, or free market utopias popularized in the Anglo-American world in the 1980s. (Dryzek 1997: 192)

The exact structure and nature of any new system cannot be predicted; how it manifests itself (if at all) will be a function of how people participate in the future (Walker 1988). What follows should be seen as tentative suggestions offered as a contribution to future dialogue. It is important to note that the author's experience of Australasian political systems inevitably conditions these observations. Further, recognising that responsibility for environmental insecurity rests primarily with industrialised countries and the majority of their populations, the following discussion is biased towards reform in these places. This is not to say that reforms are not necessary in industrialising countries; the focus here, however, is on the larger source of the problem.

People and politics

A human-centred environmental security concept runs the risk of depicting people as passive recipients of strategies to enhance environmental security. Yet because human security means rethinking politics, part of the task must be to consider the role of people as actors deliberately seeking to shape social and political life; that is, as agents of security. Agency is defined as 'the power of actors to operate independently of the determining constraints of social structure ... the volitional, purposive nature of human activity as opposed to its constrained, determined aspects' (Jary and Jary 1995: 10). The difficulty with agency lies in the structure–agency dialectic. No-one is wholly autonomous from the influence of social structures and their constraining power cannot be discounted. Nevertheless, to advocate agency is to see power in a positive way as the ability of people, individually and collectively, to resist or reshape restrictive and oppressive structures.

Individuals as consumers

It was argued in the previous chapter that environmental security entails the stable provision of basic health needs. For this to occur, the relative consumption needs of wealthy people need to be curtailed, as it is the satisfaction of these, through economic and ecological processes, which exploits poorer peoples and their environs. The criterion of 'wealthy' being used here is not a numerical baseline, but rather the extent of the difference between people's material circumstances; after all, wealth and poverty are relative phenomena. By this measure, applied globally, the average middle-class person in a Western liberal democracy is inordinately wealthy. Much of the dilemma of consumption stems from the comparison of oneself to those who have more, rather than to those who have less: we tend to think in terms of our relative poverty rather than our relative wealth, and correspondingly seek to 'keep up' rather than appreciate what we have relative to others. The truly wealthy have the freedom to choose their lifestyles; as well as bearing the most moral responsibility, they also have sufficient power to change patterns of consumption and production.

It has been established that excess consumption elicits a more elaborate set of needs, thereby perpetuating a wasteful consumption/satisfaction cycle (Adorno and Horkheimer 1979). For Marcuse, excess consumption suppresses people's real needs and creates a 'false consciousness', and so 'the prevalence of repressive needs is a fact that must be undone in the interests of the happy individual as well as all those whose misery is the price of his satisfaction' (Marcuse 1964: 5). It follows, then, that people can satisfy their interests, and protect the material conditions of others, by changing their way of life.

More recently, empirical studies have supported the understanding that consumption of luxury or non-basic goods and services is fuelled by the relativity of status that this confers. In 1990 *The Economist* noted that while per capita income in the United States had steadily increased since 1973, middle-class Americans nevertheless perceived that living standards had stagnated or fallen (*The Economist* 1990). The implicit message was that the pleasure obtained from consumption had decreased, suggesting that consumer satisfaction is a relative phenomenon. People consume because others around them do (Scitovsky 1976). It therefore 'cannot be demonstrated that consuming more makes the representative individual happier' (Common 1996: 15). This exposes the fallacy of conventional economic, political and cultural wisdom which (erroneously) holds that more goods and services means more Good.

Making the environmental dimension of this wealth/well-being paradox more explicit, Dovers (1994: 23) plots the UNDP's Human Development Index (itself an expression of the disjuncture between wealth and welfare) against energy use for certain countries. Dovers finds that gains in human development diminish above a certain level of energy use. Some countries are therefore able to deliver high levels of human well-being with relatively low levels of energy consumption. This is done through a diversification of economic, social and political systems which allow welfare and well-being to be delivered by means other than increased consumption (Dovers 1994).

There are four key implications of this consumption/well-being paradox. First, the present consumer culture in the industrialised world is not merely ecologically destructive; it is also counterproductive to the genuine well-being of consumers. Second, welfare and well-being are better met (both ecologically and experientially) through the satisfaction of basic social needs such as friends, family and creative expression. Historically, these were the means to psychological health and satisfaction, and excess consumption is a hollow substitute for these more fundamental and ecologically sustainable needs. Third, the claim that economic growth is the means to deliver greater satisfaction is unmasked, and 'if growth does not deliver, then compromising it in order to protect the environment ... is much less of a problem' (Common 1996: 15). In essence, then, that consumption and growth do not enhance the Good means that the core economic tenets of modernity are flawed. Finally, because the extent of people's consumer aspirations are determined by the amount others have, aspirations to consumption will decrease overall if the standard of consumption in the industrialised countries is lower.

This consumption/well-being paradox has profound implications for the behaviour of individuals in industrialised societies. First, it suggests that working more to earn more is counterproductive to happiness as it entails sacrificing the time required to meet basic social needs in return for more (less satisfying) consumer power. This is commonly expressed in the recognition of workers that they do not get as much 'quality time' with their friends and families as they would like. Second, seeking to meet basic social needs in lieu of greater consumption means consuming fewer resources and demanding fewer products whose manufacture pollutes the environment and exploits labour; hence Gandhi's observation that 'if each retained possession only of what he needed, no one would be in want, and all would live in contentment' (Gandhi 1951: 46). Third, in terms of unemployment, the present trend of fewer people doing more work does not serve the interests of workers, and it deprives the unemployed of potential employment opportunities (Rees and Rodley 1993). The policy implication is to reduce working hours to create more jobs and enhance quality of life. Thus the motivation for individuals as agents of security (through political action) stems both from a responsibility to the Other and from an awareness that more goods does not mean more Good.

Individuals as agents

In that consuming less is a rejection of the power of the market to influence behaviour, it is a profoundly political act. In addition there are other, more explicitly political acts that individuals can and do undertake regularly. The idea that individuals can be conscious political agents begins with the recognition that politics is much more than what occurs among and between political parties and legislative bodies. Political activity includes a diverse array of actions: community organising, court actions, education initiatives, demonstrations, boycotts, working with the disadvantaged, strikes, and even the simple but profound act of conversation (see Dobson 1992, Dryzek 1997, Walker 1988). Perhaps as a function of globalisation, people are increasingly behaving as active participants in events that affect their own and others' lives (at least in Western liberal democracies). Many are moving beyond passive consumption to deliberate action, and are deliberately seeking to acquire a political identity (Rees 1991: 43), or embarking on what Bookchin calls the pursuit of selfhood (Bookchin 1982: 70).

This conscious political behaviour has been labelled 'life politics' by Giddens, who sees it as a means for (Western and middle-class) people to redress the ontological insecurity and existential anxieties they experience in late modernity (Giddens 1991). The individual's pursuit of politics is therefore about seeking influence over structures that are, in the late-modern and globalisation context, 'global in their consequences and implications' (Giddens 1991: 2). In short, this process of purposeful agency is about influencing structures to enhance the lives of the agents themselves at the same time as enhancing the lives of others.

The impetus for conscious political agency stems in part from the limitations of existing structures of governance and the dominance of formal politics. There is a growing consciousness that by voting every two or three years people are acquiescing in their own disempowerment, ironically in the name of democracy, and that politics and democracy should entail more than this. Hence more active individual participation is a manifestation of the need for a greater 'personification' of politics (Bookchin 1982: 335). In the longer term, this holds the promise of reforming existing, repressive political institutions as it generates new and legitimate structures of authority and governance.

Despite the powerful simplicity of the basic idea that people can take charge, the process is far from easy. Perhaps the greatest impediment is that alternative paths and lifestyles are hard to see. It is difficult to picture alternatives because what we see to be possible is to a large degree conditioned by experience. Thinking seriously about escaping the modern system therefore involves engaging in intensely difficult questions about possible futures; it 'is to enter upon very difficult conceptual terrain ... to move from what is to what might be ... to strain the limits of prevailing categories and to wrench enormously influential concepts out of their present contexts' (Walker 1988: 142). A collective and sustained effort at imagination is required.

A second impediment is that of technological entrapment, or what Boyden calls 'technoaddiction', which is 'the tendency of human populations to become dependent for health and survival on technological devices which were not necessary for health and survival when they were first introduced' (Boyden et al. 1990: 336). The concept is not hard to grasp but has profound importance. Put as a question, it asks *what can we do without?* Achieving environmental security involves finding substitutes for the ecologically and socially damaging technologies to which modern societies are addicted. This is a question for social policy and technology, but the impetus for reform must come from a general public demand for alternatives to be supplied through the market and by the state.

A third obstacle is the insufficient demonstration of the links between individuals, social structures, ecological damage and material deprivations (interdependence). As Agenda 21 noted:

There is still a considerable lack of awareness of the interrelated nature of all human activities and the environment due to inaccurate or insufficient information.... There is a need to increase public sensitivity to environment and development problems and involvement in their solutions to foster a sense of personal environmental responsibility and greater motivation and commitment towards sustainable development. (Agenda 21, 36.8, UNCED 1993)

Thus education becomes a critical factor in enhancing environmental security.

The suite of an individual's conscious political actions therefore includes consuming less, consuming with greater discernment, and being more involved in actions at all scales from local to global for human and ecological causes. Falk suggests that the secret is to begin *somewhere*: 'with a concrete and personal act, perhaps located in the mind, in one's daily routine, or in one's neighbourhood. The early acts should be close at hand, and gradually the circles of effect should be expanded' (Falk 1971: 19). Specific actions might include:

- Negotiating to work less;

- Trying to be as self-sufficient as possible by growing vegetables, rearing poultry, using home-based renewable energy sources, better housing design, recycling wastes and other permaculture activities;

- Investing in green energy and ethical portfolios, as well as seeking to exert greater control over pension schemes (a large source of floating capital – see Rifkin 1991);

- Taking public transport, cycling or walking as modes of transport;

- Spending more time with one's family and friends;

- Eating less energy- and resource-intensive foodstuffs. This entails consuming more fresh fruit, vegetables and grains, and less meat and frozen goods. It also involves selecting products with minimal packaging;

- Boycotting certain products and companies whose practices are known to be environmentally destructive and socially damaging, as well as favouring those which are cleaner, greener and more ethical;

- Supporting local employment-intensive businesses;

- Becoming involved in local politics and community support programmes (schooling, health care and housing for the homeless, for
  example), and engaging with local and global advocacy groups;

- Lobbying governments on a range of issues: for land reform programmes, for greater contributions to foreign aid, for better public
  transport, for renewable energy schemes, for reductions in the defence
  budget, for better education, for more effective environment and
  labour laws, and for the ratification and implementation of existing
  international treaties on the environment.

There is a danger in arguing for greater individual action and participation. To advocate this revitalisation of politics through the enhanced
participation of individuals is not necessarily the same as arguing for
community self-help, or an uncritical strengthening of 'civil society'.
While there is merit in the idea that communities can do more for themselves, there is also a great danger that pushing for this supports the neoliberal agenda for less government. Neoliberal economic theory advocates
smaller government and less spending on welfare, and proposes that these
responsibilities should be transferred to local communities, under the
rationale that they are more efficient. Thus there is a tendency for 'civil
society' and neoliberal advocates to be pushing for the same thing,
although the intent differs. Any discussion of the subsidiarisation of
welfare and the enhancement of civil society must be cognisant of these
confluent but dissimilar arguments, and the details of the expected contribution of different parties must always be given explicit mention.

Governance for environmental security

It is clear from previous chapters that the nation-state cannot be allowed
to continue to appropriate environmental security to perpetuate its own
power and to forestall genuine action on environmental insecurity.
Exposing this appropriation is the most valuable function of critical
environmental security analyses. Nevertheless, the nation-state is still the
most powerful of all formal political institutions, so efforts to enhance
environmental security through a global-scale and inclusive system of
governance will be more effective and more rapid if the nation-state acts
as a facilitator. Thus governance here means not the 'governance without

government' of Rosenau and Czempeil (1992) but good governance through governments. Good governance and global governance are not so much established realities as concepts which offer some promise of a better future.

The general thrust of the following discussion is to advocate the distribution of political power to those institutions and groups which are most capable of acting to enhance environmental security. This involves more than simply shifting authority to lower-level institutions; it also involves enhancing the authority of global institutions, non-governmental organisations, and critical social movements. This power-shifting strategy involves moving beyond the jigsaw-like political geography of the modern world where virtually all space is sovereign and boundaries are fixed. A new politics for a new conception of security means imagining an inclusive, issue-sensitive, adaptive, deterritorialised and multi-layered system of governance by people and for people. Ultimately what is necessary is full or partial dissolution of national power through progressive relinquishment of that power. In this vision the nation-state is a broker, facilitator and conduit for a new governance and politics for human and environmental security. The state as a conduit in this sense means facilitating governance from below – that is, fostering bottom-up representation of people from the local through to the global level, but at the same time enhancing the authority of coordinating institutions. This is the inverse of the present trend, noted by O'Tuathail *et al.* (1998), whereby the state increasingly acts as a conduit for exclusively top-down implementation of the rules and requirements of the global economy.

There is a growing body of literature on the meaning and practice of 'good governance', although much of what has been written about good governance is rather more about *less government* (as in the World Bank's agenda), or about *Western government* (as in the Commission on Global Governance report) (see Baxi 1996, Smouts 1998). Nevertheless, in so far as persistent human insecurity stems from a failure of political systems, Good governance (the capital 'G' hereafter denotes 'humane and effective' rather than the World Bank's 'less') is essential for the eradication of poverty, reducing environmental degradation, and increasing the welfare of people. Good governance is therefore necessary for environmental security. By Good governance, this book is referring to a system characterised by: participation and inclusion of a diversity of actors, negotiation, accommodation, coordination, responsiveness, strategic vision, respect for human rights, adaptability, flexibility, receptiveness to global and local requirements, and meeting the needs of the most deprived (after Falk 1987, Haas and Haas 1995, Smouts 1998, UNDP 1997). These are all mutually reinforcing and interdependent. Consistent with the argument made in Chapter 8, a more diverse array of institutions involved in governance enhances the resilience and adaptability of the process.

The notion of Good governance assumes the need for democracy. Although a contestable concept, democracy entails both the representation of diverse interests and the public resolution of disputes through dialogue and negotiation as opposed to force. There is no ideal and perfect system of governance, and certainly most current democratic systems are less than ideal (largely because the principles of inclusion and dialogue are not fully upheld). Nevertheless, the aim of revitalising politics and alleviating poverty would be almost impossible to accomplish in an autocratic political system. As Giddens (1994) notes, despite its flaws, democracy is the best system there is at present.

The principle of greater inclusion of alternative perspectives is integral to the notion of governance. Allowing for different values and interests, it can still be assumed that the majority will share a sense of what is Good – and this assumption seems to be supported by most NGOs and civil society groups. Arguably, such an assumption underlies most theories which advocate greater inclusion and conversation in political processes, including Habermas's communicative action (1990), Dryzek's discursive democracy (1990), and Giddens's dialogic democracy (1994). One expression of this assumption is that more participatory forms of governance mean more environmental security.

A crucial consideration for improving governance is the reform of domestic political systems to encourage participation and to create multiple channels for input into the making of policy. This is a complex area, but the general direction should be towards facilitating fair, equal and effective representation of women, children, ethnic groups, environmental organisations, labour organisations and others on a permanent basis, with flexible mechanisms to accommodate issue-based groups in particular circumstances. This entails more forums for debate and negotiation beyond political parties and the legislature, such as public debates, symposia, local parliaments, youth and NGO parliaments, broad-based policy advisory bodies, referenda, and any further opportunities for people to participate in the running of the state. Designing a wide array of mechanisms through which people can participate is a challenge for Good governance.

A fair system of governance would have equal participation from men and women at all levels, including the legislature and the public service. It is also vital that indigenous people have a greater and more formal say in governance. At a minimum, indigenous people should be given a set number of seats in decision-making and legislative bodies. Even 5 per cent of seats would increase lobbying power and make indigenous concerns heard. Of course, indigenous people should be represented proportionally, but in states where they are a minority and do not have a voice, the above recommendation would ensure a minimum standard of access.

More autonomous local-level governance is necessary if people are to participate directly in resolving issues which affect them intimately. Local governments are key players in empowering people and in facilitating the social and infrastructural requirements to enhance community resilience. Local governments are frequently (although not always) effective environmental stewards, and are well positioned to observe the social and environmental effects of private enterprise. They also help to ensure that developments within their jurisdiction have the approval and meet the needs of local people. Local governments must ensure, however, that developments within their jurisdiction do not harm others in more distant places; this is why a monopoly of authority at the local level is undesirable and higher-level coordination is required. Nevertheless, because most things happen in specific locales, Good governance is needed at the local level.

This principle of greater participation implicitly informs the trend toward greater community involvement in environmental (and cultural heritage) management in Australia. The success of Australia's Landcare movement, which has some 4,000 district-scale groups engaged in education, investigation and demonstration, is contingent upon the active involvement of a diverse range of people who have a stake in the reversal of land degradation (Martin and Woodhill 1995). A philosophy of inclusion also underlies other environmental management processes such as Total Catchment Management, environmental policy formulation processes such as the National Rangelands Strategy, and environmental management institutions such as the Great Barrier Reef Marine Park Authority (Dovers 1998). These processes mirror the intent and illustrate the difficulties of involving a diverse range of interest groups in governance processes. One of the principal difficulties is the absence of a sophisticated dialogue on goals and values. Recent research suggests that if there is to be a more diverse range of inputs into environmental governance, there needs to be enhanced dialogue about what is to be governed and for whom (Ellemor 1999). Although the principle of inclusion underlies these innovative processes, the theoretical justification is generally absent, and the coordination of efforts is generally very poor. It is interesting that in these instances practice is leading theory; nevertheless, more theoretical awareness can enhance practice.

Social movements

One of the positive aspects of globalisation is the 'bottom-up' proliferation of social movements. These are 'an assemblage of individuals linked intersubjectively to one another, based on shared identity and a common fabric of relations and practices' with 'some degree of collective consciousness' (Latham 1996: 101). The upsurge of citizen action through these groups has been a notable feature of political life and environmental restoration initiatives in recent times. The phenomenon has caught the attention of critical theorists, including Habermas, who identifies these groups as carriers of a communicative ethic, not least because they tend to debate their identity, negotiate their actions, hold to the principles of free discourse, and are not interested in reaching power but in redistributing it (Habermas 1981). Giddens says the value of social movements lies in their 'remoralization of a sphere of life denuded of moral meaning' (1985: 320), and Beck identifies these as 'the new constellation of a global subpolitics' which occurs outside the formal structures of governance (1996: 17).

It is tempting to identify these as the basis of 'global civil society' (Lipschutz and Mayer 1996), but the value of these groups needs to be put into perspective. First, it seems overly optimistic to talk of a global civil society when the world system is still fundamentally barbaric, and when the resources and access to political power of these groups are minute relative to the forces generating environmental insecurity (Conca 1995). Second, and depending on one's point of view, these transnational groups are not always 'civil': the US National Rifle Association, for example, has strong links to numerous other countries. Third, whatever governance may become, it is at present a long way from being firmly rooted in the deliberations of multifarious special interest groups.

The real potential of critical social movements lies in their ability to offer a collective and at times complementary grassroots perspective to nation-states – one which is consistent with global priorities (Elliott 1998). They add radically different streams of advice into the policy-making process; Pelling calls this 'a corrective influence on the polity' (1998: 11), while for Haas (1992) it is an 'epistemic' function. These groups (and NGOs) foster global awareness, dissolve national membranes, and exploit the positive aspects of communications and transport technology. Social movements are for the most part 'placeless', and in this sense they transcend the conflation of identity with territory, offering the potential for identity to come from recognising interdependence and the numerous affiliations available to all people. For their part, governments need to create channels to hear these alternative global and local perspectives, and need to commit themselves to implementing this advice. Of course, this would mean actively undermining the authority of the state and breaking the monopoly hold of state bureaucracies on policy advice, but this authority and monopoly contribute to the non-resolution of environmental insecurity.

Interstate governance

There are already in existence treaties and regular processes which enhance states' bilateral and multilateral efforts to address environmental and security issues. Beyond suggesting that these are important for environmental security, it is not the brief of this book to reiterate the need for, or to describe, these phenomena; this is done ably elsewhere (see for example Haas *et al.* 1993, Vogler 1995, Young 1994). Instead, the following discussion addresses issues to do with a global-scale and inclusive system of governance.

It is difficult to talk of global governance without first discussing 'globalisation'. Globalisation is best thought of as an analytical concept rather than a descriptive term, referring to the increasing density of interactions between societies and organisations, and the shifts in power that accompany this. The frequent use of globalisation to promote the idea of a borderless world where communities, peoples and states are equally subjected to the forces of globalisation, and are equally empowered, is misleading in the extreme. It should not be taken to infer equality or fairness. In every sector, be it economic, political, environmental or cultural, globalisation strongly tends to favour the already powerful. Nevertheless there are some positive facets, including the rise

of international non-government organisations and critical social movements, greater international involvement (sometimes) in settling regional
conflicts, and treaties, conventions and charters prepared under the
auspices of the United Nations and approved by a majority of states. On
the negative side, globalisation involves rampant and rapid transfers of
venture capital which have the power to make and break fortunes and
destabilise currencies. It involves deregulation of trade and investment,
which tends to undermine the capacity of states to protect industries and
firms which may be labour-intensive or greener than their foreign
competitors. This implies an erosion of sovereignty where arguably
sovereignty is most needed. Globalisation also means transnational flows
of pollutants, drugs and crime, and a widening gap in incomes and capabilities (UNDP 1997). Importantly, those who do not have access to
globalisation's facilitating transport and communication technologies are
experiencing a new form of deprivation and becoming part of what the
UNDP calls a 'structural underclass' (UNDP 1997: 25). Thus 'globalisation has profound implications for governance, the final impact of which
we cannot yet determine' (UNDP 1997: 24). In this new climate the
state must strike balances between global influences and global and local
responsibilities.

It is important not to overstate the importance of global institutions for
environmental security. Talking of the 'global' tends to obscure causes
and effects, and displace responsibilities. Action for environmental
security begins at home. If a prioritised order of action is necessary, the
rule of thumb would be: the closer to the ground, the more important the
implementation. By this token, global-level initiatives come last in
importance, and individual action in the context of global issues (act local,
think global) is the most important. Further, talking about global institutions runs the risk of proposing to centralise power, which is another
reason why power should be dispersed downwards wherever appropriate.
It should always be borne in mind that the most basic function of global
institutions is to coordinate, not enforce the actions of more localised
forms of governance. Indeed, this is true for all institutions of governance
above the local level.

The notion of global governance is unavoidable here. Global governance is posited as a means to restrain and order the unruly force of
globalisation; it is thus understood as 'systems of rule at all levels of human
activity – from the family to the international organisation – in which the

pursuit of goals through the exercise of control has transnational reper-
cussions' (Rosenau 1995: 13). This does not imply world government,
nor does it imply hierarchy as a necessary condition. The preferred term
here is *steering*, which highlights a purposefulness of governance without
presuming the need for hierarchies (Rosenau 1995). This notion of
steering is consistent with the suggestion that the function of more aggregated governance institutions is to coordinate the actions of more localised
forms of governance, not least because legitimate governance is more
likely to be achieved by bottom-up rather than top-down processes.

The best approach to a global-scale and inclusive system of governance is to build on those mechanisms already in place. The United
Nations is obviously important, and its contribution should come not so
much through the Security Council as through agencies such as the High
Commissioner for Refugees and the High Commissioner for Human
Rights; indeed, these are arguably more important for human security
than the Security Council. The general international dimension and
impartiality of these latter institutions make them unique. Enhancing
their efficacy is invaluable to the cause of environmental security. This
implies that nation-states should fund and supply personnel to these
institutions.

Enhancing good global governance requires the involvement of intergovernmental international organisations to initiate, advise and assist in
the implementation of reforms. There must be some scope for these
organisations to engage in quasi-enforcement of treaties and conventions
(Sands 1993). Intergovernmental international organisations are also
valuable for their ability to bring together NGOs, national governments,
local governments and other critical social groups, as was the case at the
UNCED and HABITAT II conferences. Global institutions are also
necessary for coordinating, developing and monitoring international agreements on the environment.

Enhancing Good governance, and thus environmental security,
demands strengthening the United Nations in the short term (although
this is not necessarily an absolute or final precondition for environmental
security). First and foremost, strengthening the United Nations means
that nation-states pay their dues to it promptly and in full. Indeed, it
suggests that nation-states increase their contributions to the UN, and
that this increase comes from savings acquired through disarmament. The
Commission on Global Governance (COGG) has made a number of

suggestions for UN reform which seem valid; for one thing, it would extend to non-state actors the right to petition the Security Council on situations where the security of people is endangered. It proposes revitalising the General Assembly as the universal forum of the world's states, and strengthening the authority of the International Court of Justice (COGG 1995: 345–7, see also Timoshenko 1989). The COGG also recommends the establishment of a Demilitarisation Fund to help developing countries reduce military commitments (but the magnitude of the waste is greater in developed countries), and it proposes establishing an Economic Security Council to deliberate and regulate matters pertaining to the global economy. These seem to be valid recommendations. An Economic Security Council might also implement and steer a unilaterally applied carbon taxation system, so that exported and imported products do not escape penalties or advantages that accrue according to their environmental cost. An Economic Security Council might also be an appropriate forum for debt reduction and to elicit and administer unencumbered aid from wealthier countries. Alternatively, however, rather than having a multitude of security councils there might be no security councils, and all matters of security could be referred to the General Assembly. A further option would be to have a single 'human security' council.

If there is merit in adding more voices to political institutions at the local and national level, then there may equally be much to be gained from similar reforms at the global level. There is an array of possibilities here. Parallel assemblies to the present UN General Assembly (of states) could be developed for indigenous people, local governments, youth and NGOs (at least). Each parallel body might then converge at a grand assembly where global issues are discussed. Alternatively, a reformed General Assembly might allocate a proportion of seats to indigenous representatives, local governments, youth and NGOs. The rationale is simple: global governance must involve more voices than those of nation-states. This principle should extend into whatever 'security councils' are formed.

An important function of global governance is to regulate the environmentally and socially damaging activities of multinational corporations and transnational capital (O'Tuathail *et al.* 1998). The power of these processes and corporations should not be overstated to the point of obscuring the options available to the state. There are alternatives that arise from a fundamental difference between private multinational corporations and states, which is that states *control space*. This is not often a positive feature of states – but it forms the basis of any effective strategy to control multinational corporations and speculators, because their activities still occur somewhere. The principal difficulty rests not so much in the feasibility of control and the means to achieve it, but in the need for unilateral control across all states. In this sense coordinated and consistent global governance is particularly necessary.

It is tempting to conclude this discussion with a more concrete and confident statement about the policies and institutions of governance necessary for environmental security. The best one can do, however, is restate the informing principles required for successful and legitimate forms of governance. These are: inclusion, conversation, access, equity, and coordinated (not enforced) bottom-up processes of reform. Beyond this, all that might be said is that the issue of governance needs much further investigation.

(In)Conclusions

Conclusions imply closure, but the deeper aim of this book has been to open up the study of environmental security by thinking critically about existing approaches, and beginning to think about alternative possibilities. So it is the (in)conclusions that warrant most attention.

This book has explored the politics of security discourse as it relates to the environment. It has argued that environmental security securitises environmental problems, thereby making them more important than other mainstream political issues. This is a double-edged sword, for while securitising environmental issues risks state cooption, colonisation and emptying of the environmental agenda, it can also contest the legitimacy of the prevailing approach to security and highlight its contradictions. The latter function justifies the risks, particularly since in most respects the concept has been coopted anyway. If environmental problems can be securitised in a way that challenges the national security paradigm yet is cognisant of current policy directions, national governments may well take environmental problems more seriously, reduce defence budgets, and implement policies for a more peaceful and environmentally secure world. This book has argued that for environmental security to be competitive in this way, and for it to offer useful policy advice, it needs to be framed in terms of *human* security.

So environmental security is a risky venture, but one worth pursuing. The greatest risk, perhaps, is that the national security policy community may abandon the use of 'environmental security' altogether, thereby ending the discursive contest. Until such time, there is a need for ongoing and obstinate contestation of the meaning and practice of security and environmental security. There are three parts to this. First, there is a need for continued development of theories and explanations which can serve as solid foundations for a human-centred environmental security concept. Second, and contingent upon the former, there is a need for ongoing critique of existing theories and practices of security and environmental security. This can be done, for example, through a framework of questions – Whose security? Security from what? Insecurity how? Why security? – and by exposing contradictions between the alleged benefits of the theory and practice of environmental security and the reality of environmental insecurity. Third, and contingent upon the first two components, there is a need to posit alternative theories and concepts, and to link these to practice. In general, the critique of security and environmental security is progressing rapidly, and so the challenges lie more in developing the foundations and advancing the alternatives. The remainder of this discussion provides thoughts on ways to enhance the contestation of the meaning and practice of security and environmental security according to these three components.

One area that this book has not explored, but is necessary, is the need for alternative histories. A contention of this book (after Gandhi) is that history tends to be a ledger of anomalous episodes of conflict which is then read as proof that humans are predisposed to violence. It is thus the silences of history, those more prolific instances of negotiation and cooperation, that need to be found and asserted as these offer a basis of hope and lessons in strategy for peace and security. This calls for extensive projects on both peace histories and human–environment histories.

Because security is integral to national identity in its delineation of threatening Others (an inherently violent form of identity creation which justifies militarism), it entrenches a competitive and hostile view of the world. In such a world there can be no unilateral action to protect people and the environment. There is therefore a need to dissolve this crude identity politics. The challenge is to construct multiple maps that show the dimensions and spectrums of other political, ecological, social, economic and cultural spaces and processes. If the individual and social groups can appreciate the multiple forms of affiliation that are available to them, this might serve as a positive source of identity creation which embraces the global community and breaks down the distinction between Us and Other. Expanding awareness of the complexity and connectivity of the world may help overturn the tendency to blame risks on Others. We may then appreciate that in life there will always be insecurity and risk, but violence rarely provides security.

Scholarship of a critical nature clearly has a key role to play in enhancing environmental security. The basic function of critical scholarship is to open up thinking space and to generate alternatives. More specifically for environmental security, critical scholarship must continue to unmask discourses which construct ethnocentric and essential accounts of reality and identity, which in turn lead to practices which exclude and oppress people who lie outside the frame of reference. There is a continuing need to challenge simplistic responses to complex problems. It is also frequently necessary to challenge the presumption that economic forces are beyond political control. Further, it is necessary to go on contesting singular representations of words like security, as it is through such contestations that malignant discourses can be critiqued and alternatives proposed.

In order to enhance the robustness of its human-centred concept of environmental security, this book has drawn on elements of the theories of ecology, hazards, and environmental management and policy, in conjunction with theories of global politics. Whatever the limitations of what has been presented here, there is nevertheless a degree of confluence between these perspectives. Their integration offers one way to further the theory and practice of environmental security. Nevertheless, the problems with such an interdisciplinary approach should be considered. The environmental security literature is rife with simplifications, misconstructions and misappropriations of natural science theories by social and political scientists, and conversely of social and political theories by biophysical scientists. Thus great caution and prudence is involved, particularly when the audience contains institutions capable of waging war.

A substantial amount of the environmental security literature looks at disruptions to local environments and the ways these may induce conflict. Little consideration is given, however, to the day-to-day insecurities that people face, or to the broader global economic processes that in many direct and indirect ways generate environmental insecurity. If we are to understand the phenomenon of environmental insecurity better, these routine impacts of global processes must be known. Development studies has already provided many valuable lessons here, but this is a challenging area and understanding is not complete. A useful research strategy would be to conduct a series of case studies of environmental insecurity across a diverse range of places and cultures in an attempt to explicate both common and particular causes. As an immediate task, the lessons of similar types of analysis that are already available could be described in the language of security, so that the global–local mechanisms which generate insecurity could be brought to the fore of security discourse.

A more necessary research task is to demonstrate how people cope with vulnerability and scarcity in *peaceful* ways. This is the inverse of the many case studies attempting to link environmental degradation and violent conflict. If we are serious about peace then we should learn from instances of peace. A case-study approach like the one suggested in the previous paragraph might help elicit what is common to the many cases where people have responded non-violently to externally derived but locally felt environmental insecurity. The lessons distilled from these case studies could then be applied to cases where communication and co-operative arrangements for peace and sustainable development have broken down. A challenge for environmental security, then, is to learn from instances of cooperation rather than focusing on instances of violent conflict.

Although it is a contention of this book that peace is the best means to achieve environmental security, the various connections between peace and environmental degradation need to be explored more fully. One particularly fruitful area for research would be to investigate the possibility that common environmental problems can provide a basis for the resolution of long-standing social and political conflicts: for example, water scarcity seems to be a particularly valuable basis upon which to build peace. Thus if peace is necessary for environmental security, it is also possible that joint efforts to resolve environmental problems can build peace.

Advancing peace also demands creative and constructive engagement with the military, however difficult this might be. This might be done through careful involvement of the military in environmental restoration and (non-coercive) protection. There is clearly enormous scope for further research to develop specific programmes in which the military might be involved.

This book has argued that environmental insecurity stems from a failure of politics and governance. To this end the most important research agenda of all is to find ways to revitalise politics, and to design a polycentric, scale-varied, coordinated system of governance that is flexible and represents all people. This is an extremely difficult but essential task.

In the final analysis, enhancing environmental security involves no less than overcoming the negative aspects of modernity. This means thinking seriously about the nation-state and ways to reform it. It means resolving difficult issues to do with politics, justice, responsibility, diversity, and the situating and scaling of legitimate institutions of governance. This will not be easy but, if it has done nothing else, this book may have shown that an environmentally secure future is still a possibility.

Bibliography

Ackerman, R. (1990) 'Defense Machinery Gears up to Fight Environmental Threat', *Signal*, December, pp. 35-38.

Adorno, T. and Horkheimer, M. (1979) *Dialectic of Enlightenment*, translated by J. Cumming, Verso, London.

Albright, M. (1998) *Earth Day 1998: Global Problems and Global Solutions*. http://secretary.state.gov/www/statements/1998/980421.html

Anderson, J. (1984) *Public Policy Making: An Introduction*, Houghton Mifflin, Boston.

AODRO (Australian Overseas Disaster Response Organisation) (1991) *Weekly Summary* (6 May, 12 May, 12 June), Australian Overseas Disaster Response Organisation, Surrey Hills (NSW).

Baldwin, D. (1997) 'The Concept of Security', *Review of International Studies*, Vol. 23, No. 1, pp. 5–26.

Barnet, R. (1984) 'The Illusion of Security', in B. Weston (ed.), *Towards Nuclear Disarmament and Global Security*, Westview, Boulder, pp. 161–72.

Barnett, J. (1997) 'Fallout and Fallouts: Nuclear Power in Southeast Asia', *Contemporary Southeast Asia*, Vol. 18, No. 4, pp. 361–76.

Baxi, U. (1996) 'Global Neighbourhood and the Universal Otherhood: Notes on the Report of the Commission on Global Governance', *Alternatives*, Vol. 21, No. 4, pp. 525–49.

Beaumont, P. (1997) 'Water and Armed Conflict in the Middle East – Fantasy or Reality?', in N. Gleditsch (ed.), *Conflict and the Environment*, Kluwer Academic Publishers, Dordrecht, pp. 355–74.

Beck, U. (1996) 'World Risk Society as Cosmopolitan Society? Ecological Questions in a Framework of Manufactured Uncertainties', *Theory, Culture and Society*, Vol. 13, No. 4, pp. 1–32.

Bennett, J and Dahlberg, K. (1990) 'Institutions, Social Organisations, and Cultural Values', in B. Turner (ed.), *The Earth as Transformed by Human Action: Global and Regional Changes in the Biosphere over the Past 300 Years*, Cambridge University Press, Cambridge, pp. 69–86.

Bergin, A. (1994) *The Pacific Patrol Boat Project: A Case Study of Australian Defence Cooperation*, Australian Foreign Policy Publications Program, Australian National University, Canberra.

Bode, T. (1997) 'Address to the Earth Summit +5', Special Session of the United Nations General Assembly to Review and Appraise the Implementation of Agenda 21, New York, 23–27 June.

Bolt, R. (1992) 'Greening Australia's Security Policy', in G. Smith and St J. Kettle (eds), *Threats Without Enemies: Rethinking Australia's Security*, Pluto Press, Leichhardt, pp. 88–112.

Bookchin, M. (1982) *The Ecology of Freedom: The Emergence and Dissolution of Hierarchy*, Cheshire Books, Palo Alto.

—— (1986) *The Modern Crisis*, New Society Publishers, Philadelphia.

Booth, K. (1991) 'Security and Emancipation', *Review of International Studies*, Vol. 17, No. 4, pp. 313–26.

Borrow, D. (1996) 'Complex Insecurity: Implications of a Sobering Metaphor', *International Studies Quarterly*, Vol. 40, No. 4, pp. 435–50.

Boulding, E. (1992) *The Underside of History: A View of Women Through Time*, Vol. 2, Sage, California.

—— (1988) *Building a Global Civic Culture: Education for an Interdependent World*, Teachers College Press, New York.

Boyden, S. (1987) *Western Civilisation in Biological Perspective: Patterns in Biohistory*, Oxford University Press, New York.

Boyden, S. and Dovers, S. (1997) 'Humans in the Biosphere', in M. Diesendorf and C. Hamilton (eds), *Human Ecology, Human Economy: Towards an Ecologically Sustainable Society*, Allen and Unwin, Sydney, pp. 3–34.

Boyden, S., Dovers, S. and Shirlow, M. (1990) *Our Biosphere Under Threat: Ecological Realities and Australia's Opportunities*, Oxford University Press, Melbourne.

Brock, L. (1991) 'Peace Through Parks: The Environment on the Research Agenda', *Journal of Peace Research*, Vol. 28, No. 4, pp. 407–23.

—— (1992) 'Security Through Defending the Environment: An Illusion?', in E. Boulding (ed.), *New Agendas for Peace Research: Conflict and Security Reexamined*, Lynne Rienner, Boulder, pp. 79–102.

—— (1996) 'The Environment and Security – Conceptual and Theoretical Issues', paper read at the 16th General Conference of the International Peace Research Association, July, University of Queensland.

—— (1997) 'The Environment and Security: Conceptual and Theoretical Issues', in N. Gleditsch (ed.), *Conflict and the Environment*, Kluwer Academic Publishers, Dordrecht, pp. 17–34.

Brown, L. (1977) *Redefining National Security*, Worldwatch Paper No. 14, Worldwatch, Washington.

Brown, L., Flavin, C. and Kane, H. (1996) *Vital Signs 1996–1997: Trends That Are Shaping Our Future*, Earthscan, London.

Brown, L., Renner, M. and Flavin, C. (1998) *Vital Signs 1998: The Environmental Trends That Are Shaping Our Future*, W.W. Norton and Company, London and New York.

Bullard, R. (ed.) (1994) *Unequal Protection: Environmental Justice and Communities of Colour*, Sierra Club Books, San Francisco.

Bulloch, J. and Darwish, A. (1993) *Water Wars: Coming Conflicts in the Middle East*, Victor Gollancz, London.

Bush, G. (1990) *National Security Strategy of the United States 1990–1991*, Brassey's, Washington.

Butts, K. (1994) 'Why the Military is Good for the Environment', in J. Kakonen (ed.), *Green Security or Militarized Environment*, Dartmouth, Aldershot, pp. 83–109.

Buzan, B. (1991) *People, States and Fear: An Agenda for International Security Studies in the Post-Cold War Era*, Harvester Wheatsheaf, Hertfordshire.

Byers, B. (1991) 'Ecoregions, State Sovereignty and Conflict', *Bulletin of Peace Proposals*, Vol. 22, No. 1, pp. 65–76.

—— (1994) 'Armed Forces and the Conservation of Biodiversity', in J. Kakonen (ed.), *Green Security or Militarized Environment*, Dartmouth, Aldershot, pp. 111–30.

Campbell, A. (1994) *Landcare: Communities Shaping the Land and the Future*, Allen and Unwin, Sydney.

Campbell, D. (1992) *Writing Security: United States Foreign Policy and the Politics of Identity*, Manchester University Press, Manchester.

—— (1993) *Politics Without Principle: Sovereignty, Ethics, and the Narratives of the Gulf War*, Lynne Rienner, Boulder.

Carr, E. (1939) *The Twenty Years' Crisis, 1919–1939: An Introduction to the Study of International Relations*, Macmillan, London.

Carroll, J. (1989) 'The Acid Challenge to Security', *Bulletin of Atomic Scientists*, Vol. 45, No. 8, pp. 32–4.

Cheeseman, G. (1995) *Structuring the ADF for UN Operations: Change and Resistance*, Australian Defence Studies Centre Working Paper no. 34, Canberra.

Cherry, W. (1996) 'Human Rights and Environmental Security: Forging the Links', paper read at the 16th General Conference of the International Peace Research Association, July, University of Queensland.

Christopher, W. (1996) *American Diplomacy and the Global Environmental Challenges of the 21st Century*, Address at Stanford University, 9 April 1996. http://dosfan.lib.uic.edu/text.html

Claussen, E. (1995) 'Environment and Security: The Challenge of Integration', *Environmental Change and Security Project Report*, No. 1, pp. 40–3.

Clements, K. (1990) *Towards a Sociology of Security*, Working Paper No. 90-4, Conflict Resolution Consortium, University of Colorado, Boulder.

Clinton, W. (1995a) 'Remarks on Earth Day 1994', excerpts in *Environmental Change and Security Project Report*, No. 1, p. 51.

—— (1995b) 'National Security Strategy of Engagement and Enlargement', excerpts in *Environmental Change and Security Project Report*, No. 1, pp. 47–50.

—— (1998) *A National Security Strategy for a New Century*, The White House, Washington.

COGG (The Commission on Global Governance) (1995) *Our Global Neighbour-hood: The Report of the Commission on Global Governance*, Oxford University Press, Oxford.

Cohn, J. (1996) 'New Defenders of Wildlife', *BioScience*, Vol. 46, No. 1, pp. 11–14.

Common, M. (1995) *Sustainability and Policy: Limits to Economics*, Cambridge University Press, Cambridge.

—— (1996) 'What is Ecological Economics?', in R. Gill (ed.), *R&D Priorities for Ecological Economics*, Land and Water Resources Research and Development Corporation, Canberra, pp. 6–20.

Common, M. and Perrings, C. (1992) 'Towards and Ecological Economics of Sustainability', *Ecological Economics*, No. 6, pp. 7–34.

Commonwealth of Australia (1992) *Australia's Environment: Issues and Facts*, Australian Government Publishing Service, Canberra.

—— (1993) *Are You Alert to Quarantine?*, Australian Government Publishing Service, Canberra.

—— (1994) *Defending Australia: Defence White Paper 1994*, Australian Government Publishing Service, Canberra.

—— (1996) *Australian Defence Homepage*. http://www.adfa.oz.au/DOD/dodhmpgn.html

Conca, K. (1994a) 'Rethinking the Ecology–Sovereignty Debate', *Millennium: Journal of International Studies*, Vol. 23, No. 3, pp. 701–11.

—— (1994b) 'In the Name of Sustainability: Peace Studies and Environmental Discourse', in J. Kakonen (ed.), *Green Security or Militarized Environment*, Dartmouth, Aldershot, pp. 7–24.

—— (1994c) 'Peace, Justice, and Sustainability', *Peace Review*, Vol. 6, No. 3, pp. 325–31.

—— (1995) 'Greening the United Nations: Environmental Organisations and the UN System' *Third World Quarterly*, Vol. 16, No. 3, pp. 441–57.

Cooksey, R. (1988) *Review of Australia's Defence Facilities*, Australian Government Publishing Service, Canberra.

Cooley, J. (1984) 'The War Over Water', *Foreign Policy*, No. 54, pp. 3–26.

Correia, F. and da Silva, J. (1997) 'Transboundary Issues in Water Resources', in N. Gleditsch (ed.), *Conflict and the Environment*, Kluwer Academic Publishers, Dordrecht, pp. 315–34.

Crick, B. (1993) *In Defence of Politics*, revised edition, Penguin, New York.

Dabelko, G. and Dabelko, D. (1995) 'Environmental Security: Issues of Conflict and Redefinition', *Environmental Change and Security Project Report*, No. 1, pp. 3–13.

Dabelko, G. and Simmons, P. (1997) 'Environment and Security: Core Ideas and US Government Initiatives', *SAIS Review*, Vol. 17, No. 1, pp. 127–46.

Dalby, S. (1990a) *Creating the Second Cold War: The Discourse of Politics*, Pinter, London.

—— (1990b) 'American Security Discourse: The Persistence of Geopolitics', *Political Geography Quarterly*, Vol. 9, No. 2, pp. 171–88.

—— (1991) *Rethinking Security: Ambiguities in Policy and Theory*, Peace Research Centre Working Paper No.105, Australian National University, Canberra.

—— (1992) 'Ecopolitical Discourse: "Environmental Security" and Political Geography', *Progress in Human Geography*, Vol. 16, No. 4, pp. 503–22.

—— (1994) 'The Politics of Environmental Security', in J. Kakonen (ed.), *Green Security or Militarized Environment*, Dartmouth, Aldershot, pp. 25–53.

—— (1995) 'Security, Intelligence, the National Interest and the Global Environment', *Intelligence and National Security*, Vol. 10, No. 4, pp. 175–97.

—— (1996a) 'The Environment as Geopolitical Threat: Reading Robert Kaplan's "Coming Anarchy"', *Ecumene*, Vol. 3, No. 4, pp. 471–96.

—— (1996b) 'Continent Adrift: Dissident Security Discourse and the Australian Geopolitical Imagination', *Australian Journal of International Affairs*, Vol. 50, No. 1, pp. 59-75.

—— (1997) 'Contesting an Essential Concept: Reading the Dilemmas in Contemporary Security Discourse', in K. Krause and M. Williams (eds), *Critical Security Studies: Concepts and Cases*, University of Minnesota Press, Minneapolis, pp. 3–31.

—— (1998a) 'Geopolitics and Global Security: Culture, Identity and the "POGO Syndrome"', in G. O'Tuathail and S. Dalby (eds), *Rethinking Geopolitics*, Routledge, London, pp. 295–313.

—— (1998b) 'Ecological Metaphors of Security: World Politics in the Biosphere', *Alternatives: Social Transformation and Humane Governance*, Vol. 23, No. 3, pp. 291–319.

—— (1999) 'Threats from the South: Geopolitics, Equity and "Environmental Security"', in D. Deudney and R. Matthew (eds), *Contested Grounds: Security and Conflict in the New Environmental Politics*, State University of New York Press, Albany, pp. 155–85.

Davies, S., Leach, M. and David, R. (1991) *Food Security and the Environment: Conflict or Complementarity?* IDS Discussion Paper No. 285, Institute of Development Studies, Sussex.

Deibert, R. (1996) 'From Deep Black to Green? Demystifying the Military Monitoring of the Environment', *Environmental Change and Security Project Report*, No. 2, pp. 28–32.

Department of State (United States) (1997) *Environmental Diplomacy: The Environment and US Foreign Policy*.
http://www.state.gov/www/global/oes/earth.html

Deudney, D. (1990) 'The Case Against Linking Environmental Degradation and National Security', *Millennium: Journal of International Studies*, Vol. 19, No. 3, pp. 461–76.

—— (1991) 'Environment and Security: Muddled Thinking', *The Bulletin of Atomic Scientists*, Vol. 47, No. 3, pp. 23–8.

—— (1992) 'The Mirage of Eco-War: The Weak Relationship Among Global Environmental Change, National Security and Interstate Violence', in I. Rowlands and M. Greene (eds), *Global Environmental Change and International Relations*, Macmillan, London, pp. 169–91.

Deutch, J. (1997) 'The Environment on the Intelligence Agenda', *Environmental Change and Security Project Report*, No. 3, pp. 113–15.

de Wilde, J. (1996) 'Environmental Security Levelled Out: Tracing Referent Objects, Threats and Scales of Environmental Issues', paper read at the 16th General Conference of the International Peace Research Association, July, University of Queensland.

Dobson, A. (1992) *Green Political Thought*, Routledge, London.

DOD (Department of Defense, US) (1997) *Environmental Security Mission*, Office of the Deputy Under Secretary of Defense [Environmental Security]. http://www.acq.osd.mil/ens

—— (1999) *The Strategic Environmental Research and Development Program*. http://www.serdp.org/

Donnelly, J. (1993) *International Human Rights*, Westview, Boulder.

Doran, P. (1995) 'Earth, Power, Knowledge: Towards a Critical Global Environmental Politics', in J. MacMillan and A. Linklater, *Boundaries in Question: New Directions in International Relations*, Pinter, London, pp. 193–211.

Dovers, S. (1994) *Sustainable Energy Systems: Pathways for Australian Energy Reform*, Cambridge University Press, Cambridge.

—— (1995) 'A Framework for Scaling and Framing Policy Problems in Sustainability', *Ecological Economics*, No. 12, pp. 93–106.

—— (1997) 'Sustainability: Demands on Policy', *Journal of Public Policy*, Vol. 16, No. 3, pp. 303–18.

—— (1998) 'Community Involvement in Environmental Management: Thoughts for Emergency Management', *Australian Journal of Emergency Management*, Vol. 13, No. 2, pp. 6–11.

Dovers, S. Norton, T. and Handmer, J. (1996) 'Uncertainty, Ecology, Sustainability and Policy', *Biodiversity and Conservation*, No. 5, pp. 1143–67.

Dower, N. (1995) 'Peace and Security: Some Conceptual Notes', in M. Salla, W. Tonetto and E. Martinez (eds), *Essays on Peace: Paradigms for Global Order*, Central Queensland University Press, Rockhampton, pp. 18–23.

DPIE (Department of Primary Industries and Energy Australia) (1990) *Rehabilitation of Former Nuclear Test Sites in Australia*, Australian Government Publishing Service, Canberra.

Dryzek, J. (1990) *Discursive Democracy: Politics, Policy, and Political Science*, Cambridge University Press, Cambridge.

—— (1997) *The Politics of the Earth: Environmental Discourses*, Oxford University Press, Oxford.

Dunn, W. (1981) *Public Policy Analysis: An Introduction*, Prentice-Hall, New Jersey.

Dycus, S. (1996) *National Defense and the Environment*, University Press of New England, Hanover.

Dyer, H. (1996) 'Environmental Security as a Universal Value: Implications for International Theory', in J. Vogler and M. Imber (eds), *The Environment in International Relations*, Routledge, London, pp. 22–40.

Eckersley, R. (1992) *Environmentalism and Political Theory: Toward an Ecocentric*

Approach, State University of New York Press, Albany.

—— (1996) 'Environmental Security Dilemmas', *Environmental Politics*, Vol. 5, No. 1, pp. 140–6.

Ellemor, H. (1999) 'The Cultural Geography of Resource Management: A Case Study from Australia', paper read at the 1999 New Zealand Geographical Society Conference, 'Geography and the Millennium', July, Massey University (in proceedings).

Elliott, L. (1996) 'Environmental Conflict: Reviewing the Arguments', *Journal of Environment and Development*, Vol. 5, No. 2, pp. 149–67.

—— (1998) *The Global Politics of the Environment*, New York University Press, New York.

Enloe, C. (1990) *Bananas, Beaches and Bases: Making Feminist Sense of International Politics*, University of California Press, Berkeley.

Erikson, K. (1995) *A New Species of Trouble: The Human Experience of Modern Disasters*, W.W. Norton, New York.

Evans, D. (1990) *A Fatal Rivalry: Australia's Defence at Risk*, Macmillan, Melbourne.

Falk, R. (1971) *This Endangered Planet: Prospects and Proposals for Human Survival*, Random House, New York.

—— (1987) 'The Global Promise of Social Movements', in R. Walker and S. Mendlovitz, *Towards a Just World Order: Perspectives from Social Movements*, Butterworths, London, pp. 363–86.

Finger, M. (1991) 'The Military, the Nation State and the Environment', *The Ecologist*, Vol. 21, No. 5, pp. 220–5.

Foucault, M. (1977) *Language, Counter-Memory, Practice: Selected Essays and Interviews*, edited by D. Bouchard, Blackwell, Oxford.

Funtowicz, S. and Ravetz, J. (1991) 'A New Scientific Methodology for Global Environmental Issues', in R. Constanza (ed.), *Ecological Economics: The Science and Management of Sustainability*, Colombia University Press, New York, pp. 137–52.

Galtung, J. (1969) 'Violence, Peace and Peace Research', *Journal of Peace Research*, Vol. 6, pp. 167–91.

Gandhi, M. (1951) *Satyagraha (Non-Violent Resistance)*, Navajivan, Ahmedabad.

Giddens, A. (1984) *The Constitution of Society: Outline of the Theory of Structuration*, University of California Press, Berkeley.

—— (1985) *The Nation-State and Violence*, University of California Press, Berkeley and Los Angeles.

—— (1990) *The Consequences of Modernity*, Stanford University Press, Stanford.

—— (1991) *Modernity and Self Identity: Self and Society in the Late Modern Age*, Polity Press, Cambridge.

—— (1994) *Beyond Left and Right: The Future of Radical Politics*, Polity Press, Cambridge.

Gleditsch, N. (1994) 'Conversion and the Environment', in J. Kakonen (ed.), *Green Security or Militarized Environment*, Dartmouth, Aldershot, pp. 131–54.

Gleick, P. (1990) 'Environment, Resources, and International Security and Politics', in E. Arnett (ed.), *Science and International Security*, American

Association for the Advancement of Science, Washington, pp. 501–23.

—— (1991) 'Environment and Security: The Clear Connections', *The Bulletin of Atomic Scientists*, Vol. 47, No. 3, pp. 17–21.

—— (1993) 'Water and Conflict: Fresh Water Resources and International Security', *International Security*, Vol. 18, No. 1, pp. 79–112.

Gore, A. (1990) 'SEI: A Strategic Environment Initiative,' *SAIS Review,* Vol. 10, No. 1, pp. 59–71.

Graeger, N. (1996) 'Environmental Security?', *Journal of Peace Research*, Vol. 33, No. 1, pp. 109–16.

Gray, C. (1996) 'The Continued Primacy of Geography', *Orbis: A Journal of World Affairs*, Vol. 40, No. 2, pp. 247–59.

Gunder Frank, A. (1966) 'The Development of Underdevelopment', *Monthly Review*, Vol. 18, No. 4, pp. 17–31.

Gurtov, M. (1991) *Global Politics in the Human Interest*, Lynne Rienner, Boulder.

Haas, P. (1992) 'Obtaining International Environmental Regulation Through Epistemic Consensus', in I. Rowlands and M. Greene (eds), *Global Environmental Change and International Relations*, Macmillan, London, pp. 38–59.

Haas, P. and Haas, E. (1995) 'Learning to Learn: Improving International Governance', *Global Governance*, Vol. 1, No. 3, pp. 255–85.

Haas, P., Keohane, R. and Levy, M. (eds) (1993) *Institutions for the Earth: Sources of Effective International Environmental Cooperation*, MIT Press, Massachusetts.

Habermas, J. (1981) 'New Social Movements', *Telos: A Quarterly Journal of Radical Thought*, No. 49, pp. 33–7.

—— (1990) *Moral Consciousness and Communicative Action*, Polity Press, Cambridge.

Handmer, J. (1996a) 'Communicating Uncertainty: Perspectives and Themes', in T. Norton, T. Beer and S. Dovers (eds), *Risk and Uncertainty in Environmental Management*, Centre for Resource and Environmental Studies, Canberra, pp. 86–97.

—— (1996b) 'Issues Emerging from Natural Hazard Research and Emergency Management', in T. Norton, T. Beer and S. Dovers (eds). *Risk and Uncertainty in Environmental Management*, Centre for Resource and Environmental Studies, Canberra, pp. 44–62.

Handmer, J. and Dovers, S. (1996) 'A Typology of Resilience: Rethinking Institutions for Sustainable Development', *Industrial and Environmental Crisis Quarterly*, Vol. 9, No. 4, pp. 482–511.

Hay, C. (1994) 'Environmental Security and State Legitimacy', in M. O'Connor (ed.), *Is Capitalism Sustainable? Political Economy and the Politics of Ecology*, The Guilford Press, New York, pp. 217–23.

Harvard Working Group on New and Resurgent Diseases (1996) 'Globalization, Development, and the Spread of Disease', in J. Mander and E. Goldsmith (eds), *The Case Against the Global Economy: And for a Turn Toward the Local*, Sierra Club Books, San Francisco, pp. 160–70.

Heininen, L. (1994) 'The Military and the Environment: An Arctic Case', in J. Kakonen (ed.), *Green Security or Militarized Environment*, Dartmouth, Aldershot, pp. 155–67.

Hewitt, K. (1983) 'The Idea of Calamity in a Technocratic Age', in K. Hewitt (ed.), *Interpretations of Calamity*, Allen and Unwin, Boston, pp. 3–29.

Holling, C. (1973) 'Resilience and Stability of Ecological Systems', *Annual Review of Ecological Systems*, No. 4, pp. 1–24.

Homer-Dixon, T. (1991) 'On the Threshold: Environmental Changes as Causes of Acute Conflict', *International Security*, Vol. 16, No. 2, pp. 76–116.

—— (1992) 'Population Growth and Conflict', in E. Kirk (ed.), *Environmental Dimensions of Security: Proceedings From an AAAS Annual Meeting Symposium*, American Association for the Advancement of Science, Washington, pp. 9–16.

—— (1995) *Strategies for Studying Causation in Complex Ecological-Political Systems*, American Association for the Advancement of Science, Toronto.

Homer-Dixon. H and Percival, V. (1996) *Environmental Scarcity and Violent Conflict: Briefing Book*, American Association for the Advancement of Science, Toronto.

ICDSI (Independent Commission on Disarmament and Security Issues) (1982) *Common Security: A Blueprint for Survival*, Simon and Schuster, New York.

ICIDI (Independent Commission on International Development Issues) (1980) *North–South: A Programme for Survival*, Pan Books, London.

—— (1983) *Common Crisis North–South: Cooperation for World Recovery*, Pan Books, London.

ICPD (International Conference on Population and Development) (1994) *Report of the International Conference on Population and Development, Cairo 5–13 September,* United Nations Population Information Network, New York.

Imber, M. (1994) *Environment, Security, and UN Reform*, Macmillan, London.

IPCC (International Panel on Climate Change) (1995) *Summary for Policymakers: The Science of Climate Change, IPCC Working Group 1*, UK Meteorological Office, Bracknell.

Jary, D. and Jary, J. (1995) *Collins Dictionary of Sociology*, HarperCollins, Glasgow.

Jennings, P. (1997) communique issued on behalf of the Australian Minister for Defence, 4 April, Canberra.

Jervis, R. (1991) 'The Future of World Politics: Will it Resemble the Past?', *International Security*, Vol. 16, No. 3, pp. 39–57.

Kakonen, J. (1992) 'The Concept of Security – From Limited to Comprehensive', in J. Kakonen (ed.), *Perspectives on Environmental Conflict and International Politics*, Pinter, London, pp. 146–55.

Kaplan, R. (1994) 'The Coming Anarchy', *Atlantic Monthly*, Vol. 273, No. 2, pp. 44–76.

Keller, K. (1997) 'Unpackaging the Environment', *Environmental Change and Security Project Report*, No. 3, pp. 5–14.

Klein, B. (1989) 'The Textual Strategies of the Military: Or Have You Read Any Good Defense Manuals Lately?', in J. der Derian and M. Shapiro (eds), *International/Intertextual Relations: Postmodern Readings of World Politics*, Lexington Books, Massachusetts/Toronto, pp. 97–112.

Klein, B. (1997) 'Every Month is "Security Awareness Month"', in K. Krause and M. Williams (eds), *Critical Security Studies: Concepts and Cases*, University of Minnesota, Minneapolis, pp. 359–68.

Kuletz, V. (1998) *The Tainted Desert: Environmental Ruin in the American West*, Routledge, New York and London.

Latham, R. (1996) 'Getting Out From Under: Rethinking Security Beyond Liberalism and the Levels-of-Analysis Problem', *Millennium: Journal of International Studies*, Vol. 25, No. 1, pp. 77–108.

Levy, M. (1995a) 'Is the Environment a National Security Issue?', *International Security*, Vol. 20, No. 2, pp. 35–62.

—— (1995b) 'Time for a Third Wave of Environment and Security Scholarship?', *Environmental Change and Security Project Report*, No. 2, pp. 44–6.

Libiszewski, S. (1997) 'Integrating Political and Technical Approaches: Lessons from the Israeli–Jordanian Water Negotiations', in N. Gleditsch (ed.), *Conflict and the Environment*, Kluwer Academic Publishers, Dordrecht, pp. 385–402.

Linklater, A. (1995) 'Neo-realism in Theory and Practice', in K. Booth and S. Smith (eds), *International Relations Theory Today*, Polity Press, Cambridge, pp. 251–4.

Lipschutz, R. (1992a) 'Reconstructing World Civic Politics', *Millennium: Journal of International Studies*, Vol. 21, No. 3, pp. 389–420.

—— (1992b) 'What Resource will Matter? Environmental Degradation as a Security Issue', in E. Kirk (ed.), *Environmental Dimensions of Security: Proceedings From an AAAS Annual Meeting Symposium*, American Association for the Advancement of Science, Washington, pp. 1–8.

—— (1995) 'On Security', in R. Lipschutz (ed.), *On Security*, Columbia University Press, New York, pp. 1–23.

Lipschutz, R. and Holdren, J. (1990) 'Crossing Borders: Resource Flows, the Global Environment and International Stability', *Bulletin of Peace Proposals*, Vol. 21, No. 2, pp. 121–33.

Lipschutz, R. and Mayer, J. (1996) *Global Civil Society and Global Environmental Governance: The Politics of Nature from Place to Planet*, State University of New York Press, Albany.

Little, W., Fowler, H. and Coulson, J. (1973) *The Shorter Oxford English Dictionary*, Oxford University Press, Oxford.

Llamas, M. (1997) 'Transboundary Water Resources in the Iberian Peninsula', in N. Gleditsch (ed.), *Conflict and the Environment*, Kluwer Academic Publishers, Dordrecht, pp. 335–54.

Lonergan, S. (1997) 'Water Resources and Conflict: Examples from the Middle East', in N. Gleditsch (ed.), *Conflict and the Environment*, Kluwer Academic Publishers, Dordrecht, pp. 375–84.

Lorenz, F. (1994) 'Environmental Issues in the Conduct of Military Operations', in H. Smith (ed.), *The Force of Law: International Law and the Land Commander*, Australian Defence Studies Centre, Canberra, pp. 143–69.

Lowi, M. (1996) 'Water Disputes in the Middle East', *Environmental Change and Security Project Report*, No. 2, pp. 5–8.

Luckham, R. (1987) *Disarmament and Development: A Survey of the Issues*, Peace Research Centre Working Paper No. 22, Australian National University, Canberra.

MacDonald, G (1995) 'Environmental Security,' *IGCC Policy Brief* 1 (February), pp. 1–4.

Maddock, R. (1995) 'Environmental Security in East Asia', *Contemporary Southeast Asia*, Vol. 17, No. 1, pp. 20–37.

Magno, F. (1997) 'Environmental Security in the South China Sea', *Security Dialogue*, Vol. 28, No. 1, pp. 97–112.

Mandel, R. (1994) *The Changing Face of National Security: A Conceptual Analysis*, Greenwood Press, Westport.

Marcuse, H. (1964) *One Dimensional Man: Studies in the Ideology of Advanced Industrial Society*, Beacon Press, Boston.

Martin, P. and Woodhill, J. (1995) 'Landcare in the Balance: Government Roles and Policy Issues in Sustaining Rural Environments', *Australian Journal of Environmental Management*, Vol. 2, No. 3, pp. 173–83.

Martin, W., Imai, R. and Steeg, H. (1996) *Maintaining Energy Security in a Global Context*, The Trilateral Commission, New York.

Maslow, A. (1954) *Motivation and Personality*, Harper, New York.

Mathews, J. (1989) 'Redefining Security', *Foreign Affairs*, Vol. 68, No. 2, pp. 162–77.

—— (1993) 'Nations and Nature: A New View of Security', in G. Prins (ed.), *Threats Without Enemies: Facing Environmental Insecurity*, Earthscan, London, pp. 25–38.

May, E. (ed.) (1993) *American Cold War Strategy: Interpreting NSC 68*, Bedford Books of St. Martins Press, Boston.

McMichael, A. (1993) *Planetary Overload: Global Environmental Change and the Health of the Human Species*, Cambridge University Press, Cambridge.

Meadows, D., Meadows, D., Randers, J. and Behrens, W. (1972) *The Limits to Growth*, Universe Books, New York.

Miller, G. (1994) *Living in the Environment*, eighth edition, Wadsworth, Belmont.

Mische, P. (1989) 'Ecological Security and the Need to Reconceptualise Sovereignty', *Alternatives*, Vol. 14, No. 4, pp. 389–427.

Mische, P. (1991) 'The Earth as Peace Teacher', in E. Boulding, C. Brigagao and K. Clements (eds), *Peace, Culture and Society: Transnational Research and Dialogue*, Westview, Boulder, pp. 133–46.

—— (1992) 'Security Through Defending the Environment: Citizens Say Yes!', in E. Boulding (ed.), *New Agendas for Peace Research: Conflict and Security Reexamined*, Lynne Rienner, Boulder, pp. 103–19.

Morgenthau, H. (1950) *Politics Among Nations: The Struggle for Power and Peace*, Alfred A. Knopf, New York.

Morrow, R. (1994) *Critical Theory and Methodology*, Sage, Newbury Park.

Mortimore, M. (1989) *Adapting to Drought: Farmers, Famines and Desertification in West Africa*, Cambridge University Press, Cambridge.

Myers, N. (1986) 'The Environmental Dimension to Security Issues', *The Environmentalist*, Vol. 6, No. 4, pp. 251–7.

—— (1987) 'Population, Environment, and Conflict', *Environmental Conservation*, Vol. 14, No. 1, pp. 15–22.

—— (1996) *Ultimate Security: The Environmental Basis of Political Stability*, Island Press, Washington.

Naff, T. (1992) 'Water Scarcity, Resource Management, and Conflict in the Middle East', in E. Kirk (ed.), *Environmental Dimensions of Security: Proceedings From an AAAS Annual Meeting Symposium*, American Association for the Advancement of Science, Washington, pp. 25–30.

Nix, H. (1990) 'Water/Land/Life: The Eternal Triangle', in Water Research Foundation of Australia (ed.), *Jack Beale Water Resource Lecture Series 1990–1994*, Water Research Foundation of Australia, Canberra, pp. 1–11.

O'Riordan, T. and Rayner, S. (1991) 'Risk Management for Global Environmental Change', *Global Environmental Change*, Vol. 1, No. 2, pp. 91–108.

Oswald, J. (1993) 'Defence and Environmental Security', in G. Prins (ed.), *Threats Without Enemies: Facing Environmental Insecurity*, Earthscan, London, pp. 113–34.

O'Tuathail, G. and Agnew, J. (1992) 'Geopolitics and Discourse: Practical Geopolitical Reasoning in American Foreign Policy', *Political Geography*, Vol. 11, No. 2, pp. 190–204.

O'Tuathail, G., Herod, A. and Roberts, S. (1998) 'Negotiating Unruly Problematics', in A. Herod, G. O'Tuathail, and S. Roberts (eds), *An Unruly World? Globalization, Governance and Geography*, Routledge, London, pp. 1–24.

Paggi, L. and Pinzauti, P. (1985) 'Peace and Security', *Telos: A Quarterly Journal of Critical Thought*, No. 63, pp. 3–40.

Parer, W. (1998) *Coalition Spending on Renewable Energy Research and Development More Than Double Last Year of Labour*, Media Release, Ministry for Resources and Energy, Canberra.

Paterson, M. (1996) 'Green Politics', in S. Burchill and A. Linklater (eds), *Theories of International Relations*, Macmillan, London, pp. 252–74.

Pelling, M. (1998) 'Social Power, Politics and Vulnerability in Globalising Societies: Experiences from the Urban South', paper read at the Sustainability, Globalisation and Hazards Conference, May, Middlesex University.

Perry, W. (1995) *An Annual Report from the DOD to the President and Congress of the US on Environmental Security*.
http://es.epa.gov/program/p2dept/defense/ann-rpt.html

Pezzey, J. (1992) 'Sustainability: An Interdisciplinary Guide', *Environmental Values*, Vol. 1, No. 4, pp. 321–62.

Pirages, D. (1997) 'Demographic Change and Ecological Security', *Environmental Change and Security Project Report*, No. 3, pp. 37–46.

Platt, A. (1996). 'Confronting Infectious Diseases', in L. Brown (ed.), *State of the World 1996*, Earthscan, London, pp. 114–32.

Porter, G. (1995) 'Environmental Security as a National Security Issue, *Current History* (May), pp. 218–22.

Prins, G. (1990) 'Politics and the Environment', *International Affairs*, Vol. 66, No. 4, pp. 711–30.

—— (1991) 'A New Focus for Security Studies', paper read at Strategic Studies in a Changing World, Canberra, August.

—— (ed.) (1993) *Threats Without Enemies: Facing Environmental Insecurity*, Earthscan, London.

Ramachandran, K. (1991) *Gulf War and Environmental Problems*, Ashish, New Delhi.

Rayner, S. (1992) 'Cultural Theory and Risk Analysis', in S. Krimsky and D. Golding, *Social Theories of Risk*, Praeger, Westport, pp. 83–155.

Redclift, M. (1987) *Sustainable Development: Exploring the Contradictions*, Methuen, London.

Rees, S. (1991) *Achieving Power: Practice and Policy in Social Welfare*, Allen and Unwin, Sydney.

—— (1994) 'Economic Rationalism: An Ideology of Exclusion', *Australian Journal of Social Issues*, Vol. 29, No. 2, pp. 171–85.

Rees, S. and Rodley, G. (1993) 'A Proposal for the Provision of Full Employment', in S. Rees, G. Rodley, and F. Stilwell (eds), *Beyond the Market: Alternatives to Economic Rationalism*, Pluto Press, Leichhardt, pp. 222–36.

Renner, M. (1990) 'Converting to a Peaceful Economy', in L. Brown (ed.), *State of the World 1990*, W.W. Norton, New York, pp. 154–72.

—— (1991) 'Assessing the Military's War on the Environment,' in L. Brown (ed.), *State of the World 1991*, W.W. Norton, New York, pp. 132–52.

—— (1994) *Budgeting for Disarmament: The Costs of War and Peace*, Worldwatch Paper, No. 122, Washington.

—— (1997) *Fighting for Survival: Environmental Decline, Social Conflict and the New Age of Insecurity*, Earthscan, London.

Rifkin, J. (1991) *Biosphere Politics: A Cultural Odyssey from the Middle Ages to the New Age*, HarperCollins, New York.

Rogers, K. (1996) 'Environmental Cooperation: Building a Theory of Peace', *International Commission on Ecological Security Newsletter*, No. 3, p. 3.

—— (1997) 'Ecological Security and Multinational Corporations', *Environmental Change and Security Project Report*, No. 3, pp. 29–36.

Rogers, P. (1994) 'A Jungle Full of Snakes: Power, Poverty and International Security', in G. Tansey, K. Tansey and P. Rogers (eds), *A World Divided: Militarism and Development After the Cold War*, St Martin's Press, New York, pp. 1–25.

Rosenau, J. (1995) 'Governance in the Twenty-first Century', *Global Governance*, Vol. 1, No. 1, pp. 13–43.

Rosenau, J. and Czempeil, E. (1992) *Governance Without Government: Order and Change in World Politics*, Cambridge University Press, Cambridge.

Saad, S. (1995) 'For Whose Benefit? Redefining Security', in K. Conca, M. Alberty and G. Dabelko (eds), *Green Planet Blues: Environmental Politics from Stockholm to Rio*, Westview Press, Boulder, pp. 273–5.

Sachs, A. (1996) 'Upholding Human Rights and Environmental Justice', in L. Brown (ed.), *State of the World 1996*, Earthscan, London, pp. 133–51.

Sachs, W. (ed.) (1993) *Global Ecology: A New Arena of Political Conflict*, Zed Books, London.

—— (1995) 'The Sustainability Debate in the Security Age', *Development*, No. 4, pp. 26–31.

Sands, P. (1993) 'Enforcing Environmental Security: The Challenges of Compliance with International Obligations', *Journal of International Affairs*, Vol. 46, No. 2, pp. 367–90.

Saurin, J. (1996) 'International Relations, Social Ecology and the Globalisation of Environmental Change', in J. Vogler and M. Imber (eds), *The Environment in International Relations*, Routledge, London.

Schrijver, N. (1989) 'International Organisation for Environmental Security', *Bulletin of Peace Proposals*, Vol. 20, No. 2, pp. 115–22.

Scitovsky, T. (1976) *The Joyless Economy: An Inquiry into Human Satisfaction and Consumer Dissatisfaction*, Oxford University Press, New York.

Seager, J. (1993) *Earth Follies: Coming to Feminist Terms with the Global Environmental Crisis*, Routledge, New York.

—— (1995) *The State of the Environment Atlas*, Penguin Books, London.

Shaw, B. (1996) 'When are Environmental Issues Security Issues?', in *Environmental Change and Security Project Report*, No. 2, pp. 39–44.

Shaw, M. (1993) 'There is no Such Thing as Society: Beyond Individualism and Statism in International Security Studies', *Review of International Studies*, Vol. 19, No. 2, pp. 159–75.

Shrader-Frechette, K. (1995) 'Hard Ecology, Soft Ecology, and Ecosystem Integrity', in L. Westra and J. Lemons (eds), *Perspectives on Ecological Integrity*, Kluwer, Dordrecht, pp. 125–45.

Siegel, L. (1996) 'Overseas Contamination: The Pentagon's Record', *Environmental Change and Security Project Report*, No. 2, pp. 15–17.

Simmons, P. (ed.) (1996) *Environmental Change and Security Project Report*, No. 2, The Woodrow Wilson Center, Washington.

Simon, J. (1981) *The Ultimate Resource*, Princeton University Press, New Jersey.

Sivard, R. (1996) *World Military and Social Expenditures 1996*, World Priorities Inc., Washington.

Siwatibau, S. and Williams, B. (1982) *A Call to a New Exodus: An Anti-Nuclear Primer for Pacific People*, Pacific Conference of Churches, Suva.

Smil, V. (1997) 'China's Environment and Security: Simple Myths and Complex Realities', *SAIS Review*, Vol. 17, No. 1, pp. 107–26.

Smouts, M. (1998) 'The Proper Use of Governance in International Relations', *International Social Sciences Journal*, No. 155, pp. 81–9.

Social and Ecological Assessment Pty Ltd (1985) *Draft Environmental Impact Statement for Proposed Extension of the Proof and Experimental Establishment, Port Wakefield, South Australia*, Department of Defence, Canberra.

Soroos, M. (1994) 'Global Change, Environmental Security, and the Prisoner's Dilemma', *Journal of Peace Research*, Vol. 31, No. 3, pp. 317–32.

Starr, J. (1991) 'Water Wars', *Foreign Policy*, No. 82, pp. 17–36.

Stephenson, C. (1988) 'The Need for Alternative Forms of Security: Crises and Opportunities', *Alternatives*, Vol. 13, No. 1, pp. 55–76.

Stern, E. (1995) 'Bringing the Environment In: The Case for Comprehensive Security', *Cooperation and Conflict*, Vol. 30, No. 3, pp. 211–37.

Stewart, C. (1997) 'Old Wine in Recycled Bottles', paper read at the Annual

Meeting of the British International Studies Association, December, Leeds.

Stoett, P. (1994) 'The Environmental Enlightenment: Security Analysis Meets Ecology', *Coexistence*, Vol. 31, No. 2, pp. 127–46.

Tennberg, M. (1995) 'Risky Business: Defining the Concept of Environmental Security', *Co-operation and Conflict*, Vol. 30, No. 3, pp. 239–58.

The Economist (1990) 'American Living Standards: Running to Stand Still', *The Economist* (10 November), pp. 19–22.

Thomas, C. (1992) *The Environment in International Relations*, The Royal Institute of International Affairs, London.

Thomas, G. (1997) 'US Environmental Security Policy: Broad Concerns or Narrow Interests', *The Journal of Environment and Development*, Vol. 6, No. 4, pp. 397–425.

Tickner, J. (1992) *Gender in International Relations: Feminist Perspectives on Achieving Global Security*, Columbia University Press, New York.

Timoshenko, A. (1989) 'Global Ecological Security: Its International Legal Scope', *Social Sciences*, Vol. 20, No. 4, pp. 238–48.

Ullman, R. (1983) 'Redefining Security', *International Security*, Vol. 8, No. 1, pp. 129–53.

UNCED (United Nations Conference on Environment and Development) (1993) *Report of the United Nations Conference on Environment and Development, Rio de Janeiro, 3–14 June 1992*, United Nations, New York.

UNCHS (United Nations Conference on Human Settlements) (1996) *Habitat II, The United Nations Conference on Human Settlements, Istanbul 3–14 June*, United Nations, New York.

UNDP (United Nations Development Programme) (1994) *Human Development Report 1994*, Oxford University Press, New York.

—— (1996) *Human Development Report 1996*, Oxford University Press, Oxford and New York.

—— (1997) *Governance for Sustainable Human Development*, United Nations Development Program, New York.

—— (1998) *Human Development Report 1998*, Oxford University Press, Oxford and New York.

UNEP (United Nations Environment Programme) (1997) *Global Environment Outlook 1997*, Oxford University Press, New York and London.

United Nations (1997) *Earth Summit +5, Special Session of the United Nations General Assembly to Review and Appraise the Implementation of Agenda 21, New York 23–27 June*, United Nations, New York.

Vogler, J. (1995) *The Global Commons: A Regime Analysis*, Wiley, Chichester.

Waever, O. (1995) 'Securitization and Desecuritization', in R. Lipschutz (ed.), *On Security*, Columbia University Press, New York, pp. 46–86.

Walker, R. (1987) 'The Concept of Security and International Relations Theory', paper read at First Annual Conference on Discourse, Peace, Security and International Society, August, Ballyvaughan.

—— (1988) *One World, Many Worlds: Struggles for a Just World Peace*, Lynne Rienner, Boulder.

—— (1993) *Inside/Outside: International Relations as Political Theory*, Cambridge University Press, Cambridge.

—— (1995) 'History and Structure in the Theory of International Relations', in J. der Derian (ed.), *International Theory: Critical Investigations*, New York University Press, New York, pp. 308–39.

Waltz, K. (1959) *Man, the State, and War: A Theoretical Analysis*, Columbia University Press, New York.

WCED (World Commission on Environment and Development) (1987) *Our Common Future*, Oxford University Press, Oxford.

Westing, A. (1976) *Ecological Consequences of the Second Indochina War*, Almquist and Wiksell, Stockholm.

—— (ed.) (1984) *Environmental Warfare: A Technical, Legal, and Policy Appraisal*, Taylor and Francis, London.

—— (1986) 'An Expanded Concept of International Security', in A. Westing (ed.), *Global Resources and International Conflict: Environmental Factors in Strategic Policy and Action*, Oxford University Press, Oxford, pp. 183–200.

—— (ed.) (1988a) *Cultural Norms, War and the Environment*, Oxford University Press, Oxford.

—— (1988b) 'Towards Non-Violent Conflict Resolution and Environmental Protection: A Synthesis', in A. Westing (ed.), *Cultural Norms, War and the Environment*, Oxford University Press, Oxford, pp. 151–9.

—— (1989) 'The Environmental Component of Comprehensive Security', *Bulletin of Peace Proposals*, Vol. 20, No. 2, pp. 129–34.

—— (1997) 'Environmental Warfare: Manipulating the Environment for Hostile Purposes', *Environmental Change and Security Project Report*, No. 3, pp. 145–9.

Wilson, E. (1992) *The Diversity of Life*, Penguin, London.

Winnefeld, J. and Morris, M. (1994) *Where Environmental Concerns and Security Strategies Meet: Green Conflict in Asia and the Middle East*, RAND, Santa Monica.

Wirth, T. (1995) 'Sustainable Development: A Progress Report', address before the National Press Club, 12 July 1994, in *Environmental Change and Security Project Report*, No. 1, pp. 54–5.

Wolf, A., Natharius, J., Danielson, J., Ward B. and Pender J. (1999) 'International River Basins of the World', *Water Resources Development*, Vol. 15, No. 4, pp. 387–427.

Worner, M. (1991) 'Global Security: The Challenge for NATO,' in E. Grove (ed.), *Global Security: North American, European and Japanese Interdependence in the 1990s*, Brassey's, London, pp. 100–5.

WRI (World Resources Institute) (1992) *World Resources 1992–93*, Oxford University Press, New York.

Young, O. (1994) *International Governance: Protecting the Environment in a Stateless Society*, Cornell University Press, Ithaca.

Zimmerman, M. (ed.) (1993) *Environmental Philosophy: From Animal Rights to Radical Ecology*, Prentice Hall, New Jersey.

Index

land degradation 14-15, 21, 44, 52, 94, 150
land shortage 50
Landcare movement 128, 150
landmines 19
Latin America 15
Law of the Sea Convention 76
Libya 54
limits to growth 111
local impacts/issues 62, 64, 98, 102, 107, 113-14, 116, 126-7, 130, 146-7, 149, 150, 153-5, 159
logging 117

Machiavelli, Niccolò 25
MacNamara, Robert 59
malnutrition 17, 19, 21, 130, 133-4
Malthus, Thomas 14, 42, 56, 60, 66
Mandela, Nelson 64
market system 52-3, 75, 85, 99, 126, 144
Maralinga nuclear test site 95
Marcuse, Herbert 142
Marshall Islands 44, 95
Marshall Plan 31
media 48, 56
Mekong River 55
Mexico 57
Middle East 55-8, 65
migrants 38-9, 42, 48, 50, 61-2, 102, 123, *see also* refugees
military, airspace hazard created by 95; and biodiversity protection 98; budget allocations to 19, 38, 40, 44, 96-7, 137, 147; and civil defence 100-1; and Cold War 26-9, 38; constructive engagement with 159; conversion to civilian purposes 105-7, 136; culture of 57; Demilitarisation Fund proposed 155; and economic security 35-6, 43; and energy security 35; environmental agenda appropriated by 98, 105, 107, 119-20, 137, 155; environmental enforcement role 98-9, 102; environmental impact of 9, 19, 44, 92-8, 103-5, 115, 122, 136; environmental monitoring by 98-100, 102; environ-

mental recovery and protection by 9, 93 97-107, 159; and environmental security 136; environmental–military linkages 7-11, 43-5; and human security 136; militarisation 19, 50; military-industrial complex 87, 92, 95, 104, 106; and national security 26-9, 38, 40, 43, 49; and North–South domination 21-2; and Others 157; as peace planners 4; and post-Cold War new security 'threats' 33, 47; and prostitution 96; and realist school of international relations 28-9; reform of 128; and refugee 'threat' 40; resources consumed by 30, 94-5; role against environmental 'threat' 33, 38-9, 43-5, 77-80, 88, 90; and segregation 96; social impact of 96; Third World military responses to poverty and environmental insecurity 38-9; and toxic waste 95-6; US forces 19, 36, 77-85, 87, 89-91, 92-101, 103-7, 109; violence glorified by 96
modernity 1, 58-9, 65, 67-9, 112, 131-2, 134, 138-9, 143-4, 148, 160
monoculture 117
Monte Bello Islands nuclear test site 95
multinational corporations 140, 146, 155-6
Murray Darling Basin Commission 129
Myanmar 19, 96

Namibia 57
nation-state 8, 26, 29-32, 34, 36, 39, 41-2, 44-5, 48, 58, 75, 88, 91, 106, 110, 113-14, 124, 127-8, 130, 138, 147-8, 152, 154-5, 160
National Rangelands Strategy 150
national identity 124
nationalism 31-2, 34, 49, 72, 74, *see also* nation-state, national identity
nature 66-7, 86, 108-9, 129-30
neoliberalism 6, 27, 147
networks 134
New Zealand 19, 96
Nile 55-6
non-governmental organisations (NGOs)

LaVergne, TN USA
06 August 2010
192399LV00001B/40/P